Scotus for Dunces

MARY BETH INGHAM, C.S.J.

Scotus for Dunces
An Introduction to the Subtle Doctor

Franciscan Institute Publications
The Franciscan Institute
Saint Bonaventure University
Saint Bonaventure, NY 14778
2003

Cover Design: Scala

Library of Congress Card Catalogue Number:
2003102503

ISBN: 1-57659-187-5

Printed in the United States of America
Phoenix Color
Hagerstown, MD

Contents

Preface

This English introduction to the thought of John Duns Scotus by Mary Beth Ingham is a most welcome text, filling as it does a definite need. After a well-written opening chapter on the life and literary works of the Subtle Doctor, the author arranges her presentation of Scotus's principal doctrines in three core chapters. Entitled Creation, Covenant and Communion, these chapters provide excellent insight into the work of Scotus and will be quite helpful to those seeking a point of entry into his complex thought.

Although Scotus's philosophy cannot be sharply separated from his theological concerns, the chapter on creation nevertheless contains those distinctive aspects of his thought that are most philosophical in nature. The chapter on the covenant, by contrast, is primarily theological, dealing with Scotus's belief that Christ's incarnation was not primarily intended as a remedy of original sin, but intended for its own sake. Another chapter, "Communion," deals with humanity's goal as sharing the inner life of love of the Blessed Trinity and how this influences our life on earth. The final chapter, "Reading Scotus Today," shows not only the relevance but also the wisdom of rethinking the central human questions of our day in light of the assumptions that underlay Scotus's own solutions to these questions.

Not only does Ingham present these excellent thematic explications, she also provides appendices containing English versions of Scotus's writings, a wonderful resource for introducing readers to his literary style and profound thought. Gathered together in this way, they are a major contribution to academic discourse.

In a previous work, Ingham emphasized how an artistic paradigm colors the thought of Scotus: the notion of beauty as a moral category runs like a *leitmotif* throughout his ethics. Without abandoning that perspective, she now reveals how another significant aspect of the subtle Duns - namely, his Franciscan ideals - unifies his seemingly random distinctive ideas.

After reading *Scotus for Dunces: An Introduction to the Subtle Doctor*, one better appreciates why Pope Paul VI once wrote in *Alma Parens*: "Saint Francis of Assisi's most beautiful ideal of perfection and ardor of Seraphic Spirit are embedded in the work of Scotus and inflame it."

Allan B. Wolter, O.F.M.
Professor Emeritus
St. Anthony Friary
St. Louis, Missouri
April, 2003

Introduction

This book offers a basic introduction to the thought of Franciscan philosopher-theologian, John Duns Scotus. Known to history as the Subtle Doctor, Scotus has a reputation for intricate and technical reasoning. He is generally acknowledged as a difficult thinker whose ideas are neither clearly set forth nor easily followed. Scotist thought is not widely known precisely because it is so difficult to access. Some may have an idea of his isolated insights, most notably his position on the divine reason for the Incarnation, but beyond this, few other than the small circle of scholars who have mastered the thought of this late thirteenth-century Franciscan would claim to know much about an overall vision.

This text, then, is meant to be a *simple guide*, that is, an introductory presentation of both the philosophical and theological aspects of Scotist thought. It is *simple*, because I do not expect the reader to have any specialized background information on medieval philosophy or theology, on Franciscan spirituality, or on any particular systematic element needed to study the thought of such a great medieval metaphysician. It is also *simple*, insofar as I present ordinary examples to explain the more intricate distinctions found in Scotist thought. It is, however, not *simple* insofar as Scotus's insights themselves could ever be simplified. Indeed, his vision of God, reality and our relationship to both is intricate and complex. It is not possible to introduce such a thinker by reducing his thought to a simplistic rendering. In what follows, points will, at times, be explained as much as is possible (or appropriate) and still fall short of the transparency that both the author and the reader might desire.

In undertaking this book, I had one central interest. Having been struck by the centrality of beauty as a moral category in Scotus,[1] I wondered whether one might approach Scotist thought from an aesthetic interpretive angle. By taking as my starting point the centrality of beauty as key to Scotist thought, I was reminded of the aesthetic dimension in other medieval thinkers, especially men like Bonaventure. The traditions of late antiquity, influenced by Augustine's Platonism and the mystical theology of Pseudo-Dionysius, fed the development of medieval philosophy and theology through the influential 12th century School of St. Victor. The Victorines kept alive this Platonic and (what we today call) Neoplatonic tradition, adding to it a love for cosmology and study of the natural world. Their legacy was central to the brilliant work of those men living in what we call the High Middle Ages (specifically the 13th and 14th centuries) when texts of Aristotle became known in the West. Key thinkers such as Thomas Aquinas, Bonaventure and Scotus lived and wrote in a period of history that was unparalleled in terms of the confluence of spiritual, intellectual, and cultural accomplishments.

As these factors came together for me, I reflected upon the specifically Franciscan dimension that lay behind this aesthetic approach. I concluded that Scotus's identity as a Franciscan might offer a more fruitful way to approach his notoriously difficult texts and, through them, to understand his thought in a more integrated manner. This would entail viewing his intellectual achievements as central to his spiritual vision, itself an integral part of his life. It would also entail an approach that must be more thematic than systematic.

Such an approach offers several advantages. First, it does not separate the domains of philosophy from theology as vastly different and opposing areas of study. Second, it does not separate the created from the uncreated order. That is, it respects the connection that Scotus himself affirms between human knowing of the created order and human knowing of God. Third, it takes seriously the identity of Scotus as a Franciscan friar, one who followed the vision of St. Francis in his life and who saw his intellectual speculation as part of a larger spiritual journey. Finally, it does not reduce the thought of such a great mind to the imposed categories of contemporary thought, whether as philosophy or theology. So often, when we study thinkers from past ages or from other cultures, we reduce their thought to our own categories of understanding, so that we might make sense of them. This is, of course, inevitable to some extent. My attempt here is to reduce this temptation to a minimum by looking at Scotus from a vantage point that is intrinsic to his identity (his Franciscanism) rather than a vantage point that I impose from my own historical perspective.

A basic assumption, then, of this book is that the category of the *beautiful* is as foundational to Scotus as it is to Bonaventure. Reflection upon this central aesthetic reveals other aspects of Scotist thought that are seen to converge upon the beautiful, in the same way that a work of art reveals more than itself. In its relationship to the artist, first, the work of art reveals a free choice to express one's talents in this particular way. This free choice reveals the intentionality of the artist to create this particular work in precisely this particular way and at this moment in time. Second, the unity of this particular work reveals its inner harmony and dignity, both in terms of what it is in itself and in terms of the artistic intention. Finally, the work of art evokes love and delight in the onlooker or listener, who is touched by its harmony and inner integrity. Reflection upon the category of the *beautiful*, then, reveals relationships: to the artist, to the work and to the audience. These dimensions of relationship are unified in the work of art as a single individual expression of creativity.

The three themes that serve as organizational points of reference in this book are three central themes of the Christian vision. They are, therefore, also central to the Franciscan vision of reality. The themes are 1) creation, 2) covenant, and 3) communion. Around each of them we discover the sense of beauty that serves as the point of convergence for several aspects. These aspects are 1) freedom and creativity, 2) dignity and integrity,

3) rationality and order, and 4) love and delight. Each chapter looks at how these aspects are at play in Scotist thought, how they come together from this particular thematic vantage point. All aspects are present in every chapter. Thus, rather than discuss divine freedom once and then move on (as a systematic approach would), we look at divine freedom as it appears to us through creation, as it expresses itself in the covenant, and as it reaches fulfillment in communion. Dignity and integrity are examined through the metaphysical category, through the centrality of the Incarnation, and in the act of divine mercy and acceptance. Rationality and order are not seen as static categories but as dynamic threads that appear first, in reality around us; second, in divine intentionality; and finally, in complete fulfillment. Finally, love and delight appear not just in the beauty of creation, but in divine fidelity and steadfastness, and finally, in the sharing of divine communion that awaits each person.

The book's structure, then, resembles a theme and its variations. The central single insight about beauty has a theme that involves four notes (freedom/creativity; dignity/integrity; rationality/order; love/delight). Each chapter offers us a variation on the theme of beauty, not just with a re-ordering of the notes, but with a change of key. The shift from creation to covenant is a shift from nature to freedom. The shift from covenant to communion is a shift from freedom to love. Thus the harmonic music of this work moves from nature to freedom to love.

In the present volume I suggest a way in which Scotus's rich philosophical and theological legacy can be understood. This particular way requires that we take seriously his identity as a Franciscan, and that we consider the elements of his vision from that vantage point. To help make his thought concrete, select passages from his texts are provided in the appendix. Surely, at various points different readers will be frustrated that the discussion does not go into greater detail or follow the implications of a particular insight. For this reason, the final bibliography is intended to point such a reader beyond an introductory level of study toward the more intricate and developed discussions of specific elements of Scotus's vision.

After a discussion of his life and works, along with the historical context for his thought (in chapter 1), we pursue the importance of creation (in chapter 2), the centrality of the covenant and relationship (in chapter 3), and the goal of communion with one another and with God in love (in chapter 4). In this way, we might understand Scotus's contribution to contemporary reflection (chapter 5) in both its horizontal and vertical dimensions. At the base of this contribution is, I believe, a richly *aesthetic* vision of all that exists. Like Francis and Bonaventure before him, Scotus is struck by the beauty of the created order and understands its existence as gift from a loving God. The beauty of creation manifests itself both visually and through the song or canticle of the universe. This beauty sets the stage for an encounter: an encounter with this gracious God, so personally attentive and intimately present to all that is, yet so hidden and discrete. It is this God who gently calls each person to respond to goodness in love, who invites and supports each one to imitate that love in self-gift, and who ultimately graces each with eternal life in the fullness of relational communion.

Acknowledgements

This book was originally used as a text in a graduate course taught at the Franciscan Institute, St. Bonaventure, New York. I would like to thank those students who participated in that summer, 2002 course, affectionately known as *Scotus for Dunces*. Their class discussions, insightful comments and suggestions both entered the texture of the material and, from a practical perspective, helped me finish the work. Their contribution to the final product cannot be measured nor adequately rewarded. I extend my sincere thanks and deep gratitude to Bryant R. Bamba, O.F.M. Cap.; Henry B. Beck, O.F.M.; Ellen M. Brickwedde; Jim Ciaramitaro, O.F.M. Conv.; George Corrigan, O.F.M.; André José Eduvala, O.F.M. Cap.; Regina Kane, O.S.F.; Eileen Magill, O.S.F.; Jane Russell, O.S.F.; and Barbara Vano, O.S.F. I also wish to thank Brian Treanor, Ph.D., for his helpful comments on chapter 5 and Mary Meany, Ph.D., and Allan B. Wolter, O.F.M., for their helpful comments and insights on a more finished version of the entire manuscript. Fr. Allan has also graciously provided the textual material that appears in the appendices. For this and for his support over the years in my own understanding of Scotus, I am most grateful. Finally, to Margaret Carney, O.S.F., and the members of the Franciscan Institute, St. Bonaventure, New York, I extend my heartfelt thanks. To them, and to all who read this book, I wish peace and every good.

Notes

[1]A theme developed in *The Harmony of the Goodness: Mutuality and Moral Living According to John Duns Scotus* (Quincy, IL: Franciscan Press, 1996).

Chapter 1

Scotus's Life and Works

At the outset of such an introductory study, it is important to have a chapter whose purpose is to give the reader some sense of the man and the time in which he lived. This is particularly important in the present case, because, in this book, I pre-suppose that Scotus's Franciscan commitments play an enormously important role in his thought. This point has become a foundational affirmation for the present study; indeed, I have chosen to organize this book, not around the philosophical underpinnings of his writings, but rather around key insights that are central to the spirituality of the Franciscan tradition. In this first chapter, then, I sketch out the biographical information we have available, the historical context that forms the background for his thought, how he figures in the thirteenth century Franciscan theological tradition (between Bonaventure and Ockham) and, finally, how all these elements help to define what is specific about his approach to reality.

When it comes to historical figures, it is always important to have a life somewhat shrouded in mystery. Where John Duns Scotus is concerned, we have more mystery than clarity. Indeed, we have very little solid information on his life. The best scholarly guess puts his birth in Duns, Scotland, possibly in the spring of 1266. A tourist visiting Duns can see the commemorative statue in the town square, dedicated to the local hero. His childhood years leave no record of any significant events for the hagiographers to relish. There may have been a Franciscan connection in the family (an uncle or cousin) because at an early age (possibly as young as fourteen) he left home to enter the Franciscan mendicant order (Order of Friars Minor). He may have done some philosophical study near his birthplace before his teachers recognized the youth's intellectual acumen and took him to Oxford where he could study with the great masters of the order and the university.

The name of John Duns Scotus first appears in ecclesiastical records in 1291, the year of his ordination to the priesthood on March 17. As did most thirteenth century scholars (and particularly those in religious orders), John benefitted from study at the universities of Oxford as well as Paris where he incepted as Master in Theology in 1305. This event would have been the equivalent to finishing his doctorate (in the modern American system), and would have come at the end of twelve to fourteen years of formal study. His years of professional teaching were few, however. The Franciscan died on November 8, 1308 in Cologne, Germany.

Five historical dates frame our knowledge of Scotus's life: March 17, 1291 (his ordination to the priesthood in Oxford); summer, 1300 (the date he records at the beginning of the *Ordinatio*); June, 1303 (the date of a document on which his name is recorded as a member of the Franciscan community of Paris); 1305 (his inception as Master in Paris); and November, 1308 (his death in Cologne). Beyond these wide markers, we have only conjecture with which to fill in the details. Much of this conjecture is grounded on inference from one of these five dates. For instance, the record of his ordination on March 17, 1291, enables historians to suggest a birth date of spring, 1266. This conjecture is given greater probability because there had been an ordination in December 1290, for which he was apparently not eligible. Since canon law required a minimum age of twenty-five for ordination, there is good reason to conclude that Scotus celebrated his 25th birthday between December, 1290 and March, 1291.

In addition, his inception as Master in 1305, when considered in light of recorded university procedures for the thirteenth and fourteenth centuries, provides good historical ground for the conjecture that he began his formal studies of theology in 1288. Since professional university studies took from twelve to fourteen years (depending upon the university), Scotus would have had to begin prior to his ordination, unless some exception had been granted in his case. Had he entered the Franciscan novitiate in 1284 (at the age of 18, normal for that time) he would have made vows in 1285. This leaves a three-year gap in his education, between 1285 and 1288. Recent historical research points to the possible significance of the medieval mendicant orders' two-tiered educational system where Scotus is concerned. Records from the early fourteenth century indicate that Augustinians, Carmelites, Dominicans and Franciscans all had a *lectorate,* an internal training program whose purpose was to prepare men for teaching and pastoral posts. Within this religious structure, the reputation of Paris (with its university) loomed large. Accordingly, each province could send two or three men to Paris for a period of study. These men would have been chosen from within the province on the basis of their intellectual performance and potential. This *lectorate* track was distinct from the historically better-known university track, whose purpose was to prepare men for higher university positions or ecclesiastical posts.[1] Given both the possibility of such a track and, what we might conclude about Scotus's intellectual performance as a young man in Scotland or England, it is not unreasonable to suggest that he studied in this *lectorate* program in Paris sometime during these early years.[2]

The more formal university program he followed may have been similar to that of Parisian records for the early fourteenth century. If so, we can map out his years of formal training prior to incepting as Master in 1305. Scotus would have begun his formal theological training at Oxford within this university track (in 1288) with the initial status of *auditor.* This phase involved a six-year program of passive training (auditing), with three years devoted to Peter Lombard's *Book of Sentences,* followed by three years of biblical study. At the end of this phase (or in 1294), at the age of twenty-eight, Scotus would have begun the seven-year intensive baccalaurate stage, where as *bachelor*, he would have lectured on the *Sentences* as well as on the *Bible*.

Part of the standard coursework required of each student (or *bachelor*) included the lectures on Peter Lombard's *Book of Sentences*. This work, Scotus's earliest set of lectures given at Oxford possibly between 1298 and 1300,[3] is known as the *Lectura*. In 1300, he began working on a revised version of this, known as the *Ordinatio*. Scotus actually records the date when he is writing the Prologue, so we are certain of this textual dating. The term *ordinatio* is technical: it refers to the more formal, revised, and personally reviewed manuscript of the *Sentences* (that is, the version reviewed by the author himself). In finalizing such a manuscript, an author would have used some material from earlier teaching, in the way that a rough draft can be used for a final draft. The *Ordinatio* is the sort of formal text that someone prepares for a final edition.

It is not unreasonable to assume that he might have had some advance notice of his appointment to Paris (to begin in the autumn of 1302) and undertook the *Ordinatio* revisions in light of his impending move to the French university. Scotus's move would have come at the request of the Minister General, who, upon the recommendation of the General Chapter, appointed select men to the Parisian university to complete their studies. This appointment would have been significant, for it was not in view of education within the order, but in view of a more important professional university career.[4] Once in Paris, Scotus continued revising this major text and, with a different set of students, began again with his lectures on the *Sentences,* Book I. In his first year, 1302-1303, he would have participated as *bachelor* in the disputation between the Franciscan Regent Master, Gonsalves of Spain, and the Dominican Meister Eckhart.[5] Scotus's Parisian teaching also provides us with the third version of his Commentary on Lombard's *Sentences*, known as the *Reportatio Parisiensis*.

These final years of intellectual development, however, were again interrupted, this time by political events. During these years of political and ecclesiastical hostility between King Philip the Fair of France and Pope Boniface VIII, events came to a dramatic climax. In June, 1303 Philip called for a council to depose Boniface and sought the signatures of all clerics and religious in support of his effort. Because he refused to subscribe to the king's effort, Scotus was forced to abandon his studies and teaching when he and other Franciscans were sent into exile. During the next academic year (1303-1304), the best scholarly guess puts him back at Oxford (or possibly even at Cambridge)[6] where he continued to lecture and work on the *Ordinatio*. He returned to Paris sometime after April 8, 1304, when Benedict XI, Boniface's successor, lifted the ban placed on the University of Paris and the King allowed the return of those he had exiled.

The newly elected Minister General, Gonsalves of Spain,[7] announced in November, 1304 that the next Franciscan Regent Master would be John Duns Scotus. His inception as Master and his Regency began in 1305. During this time, he was able to offer only one series of disputed questions.[8] Ordinarily, this important regency appointment lasted one or two years, and in 1307 Gonsalves sent him to Cologne to oversee the teaching of Theology at that important center. Scotus would only have one complete academic year (1307-1308) in this new position because of his death in November, 1308, at the age of 42. He is buried in the Franciscan church (*Minoritenkirche*) not far from the Cologne cathedral.

To a great degree, the events of Scotus's life explain why his works have been so difficult to study and understand. Scotus's travels during his years of study and teaching, along with his early death, leave scholars with an enormous quantity of textual material in various states of completion. This textual situation accounts for the variety of scholarly opinions on Scotus's positions on important questions, not the least of which are those dealing with the nature of freedom and the way in which God relates to the created order. The complex textual situation has also been responsible in part for the negative verdict brought against him by some historians of philosophy. When scholars do not have good texts to work from, conclusions can be drawn on the basis of insufficient evidence, poor scribal recording, or false attribution. This problem, where Scotus is concerned, spanned the twentieth century, as early negative judgments slowly gave way to more nuanced and moderate interpretations, thanks to the publication of the critical edition.[9] Some issues have not been settled, despite the best efforts of scholars, and so, where Scotus is concerned, the jury is still out on some questions.

Indeed, despite the intense work of international scholars over the last thirty years, there is still lack of unanimity on the exact nature of certain teachings of the Subtle Doctor. This is particularly the case in regard to his emphasis on the will and the primacy of freedom, both for human moral life and for divine action. In brief, and depending upon whom you might read, Scotus is alternately a radical thinker who defends a wildly arbitrary view of freedom, both for God and for us, or, conversely, a thoughtful scholar who tries to reconcile apparently diverse perspectives on these key issues in order that he might save both the dignity of human choice and the central role played by the divine will in creation and salvation. Let us just note here that a serious debate continues to engage the scholarly community about the authentic positions Scotus held and taught, and upon their significance for later thinkers. Regular international congresses and conferences devote considerable attention to his work, sponsored by the International Scotistic Commission and other scholarly bodies.

Part of the medieval intellectual formation leading to the degree of Master (a terminal degree, since following the completion of all requirements, the new Master could teach at the university), every bachelor was expected to author his own commentary on the *Book of Sentences*. This standard medieval text stemmed from the work of the twelfth century student of Abelard, Peter Lombard. Lombard's *Sentences* was, quite simply, a systematic compilation of all doctrinal questions (from the nature of God to final human destiny and the beatific vision). Its methodology was that of a debate, complete with arguments for and against each position, concluding with a determination. In each question, the author would present (to the best of his ability) all relevant points regarding a given position, in as much detail as he wished. Following the laying out of the arguments, the author closed with his *determinatio*, or final verdict on the matter, followed by his own responses to the most significant points raised earlier, and now seen in light of his solution. This concluding determination was by far the most important part of the textual study: it was meant to arise logically out of the dialectic of the debate and represented the position of the bachelor writing that particular commentary. Because each bachelor could organize his own arguments, the *Sentence Commentary* gives us a glimpse of his mind at work. We are able to appreciate his particular approach, as he develops his own particular way of understanding the question, and as he gives us his answer, along with his reasons for holding it.

In addition to the required questions to be handled in the course of the work, a bachelor lecturing on the Sentences could develop any point (or sub-point) of any question, according to personal interest. In this way, each *Sentence Commentary* is a variation on the original set of questions. For example, when Scotus looks at the modes of divine action, he takes Lombard's original question "Whether God could have created things better than he did?" (*Ordinatio* I, distinction 44) and re-casts it to focus on a present, rather than a past, event. He asks, "Whether God could create things other than he has ordained them to be made?" In this way, by shifting the question from what God did in the past (at the moment of creation) to what God is able to do in the present, he reveals his interest in what the present world and the present moment reveal about God, about divine power, and divine sustaining love.

Scotus's commentaries are among the most complex we have. One reason is the triple textual situation mentioned earlier.[10] A second reason is the numerous manuscripts that must be studied to establish the critical text. But also, Scotus is an intricate and precise thinker who follows every single line of argumentation to the bitter end. He develops points and sub-arguments that most of us would not have thought about. Often he provides more compelling reasons in favor of an adversary's position than does the opponent. This tendency of his to lay out every side and every point in intricate detail is one reason why there has been and, indeed, continues to be, significant debate over his positions. One can easily conclude, on the basis of the way Scotus argues, that he is defending a position he has every intention of accepting, only to find later that he rejects it in favor of another.

Every Master had his *Sentence Commentary* available for study at the local booksellers. The most famous teachers, like Thomas Aquinas and Bonaventure (the generation of the mid-thirteenth century), had other, more mature works as well. These later works offer a much more systematic formulation of the thinker's position on key issues. Here the scholar was free to determine his own methodology and organization of the material. For a man like Thomas Aquinas, the *Summa Theologiae* or *Summa Contra Gentiles* offer the more developed positions and are far more central texts in our study today than his *Sentence Commentary*. Nonetheless, consulting his early commentary is useful when one wishes to trace the development of a position, or when we seek to identify alternate versions of an argument.

There is an analogy here for the study of Scotus, although the textual situation is not so optimistic. We can look to the *Sentence* commentaries as signposts for positions that he fills out, either more systematically or, in some cases, in slightly more detail in later works like his *De Primo Principio* (*Treatise on God as the First Principle*). And, since he traveled so much during his career, the three Sentence commentaries really do shed some light on one another. This means that we can examine his approach to the same questions at three distinct moments of his life. But a caution is important: his teaching career was relatively brief (c. 1298-1308), so there is no dramatic shift or transformation of his thought that took place. We do find, rather, small corrections and re-tooling of arguments that shed light on the direction of his reflection. However, and unlike Aquinas, his more systematic works are few.

What this means in our work on Scotus is simply this: because of his early and untimely death, the Franciscan leaves very few works in final, systematic form. In addition, because of his travels to various universities, we have several versions of the same commentary. So, for example, the *Lectura* offers the earliest version of Books I-III of the *Sentences*, given at Oxford prior to 1300. In 1300, as noted above, Scotus began the revised commentary, called the *Ordinatio*, which apparently remained the basis for the most systematic revision of his thought until the end of his life. The third version of the *Sentences*, the *Reportatio*, provides us with the possibility of two separate sets of lectures, given over (roughly) two academic years. Scotus would have nearly completed the first course cycle (Books I-IV) in the 1302-03 academic year, with the final weeks of his teaching interrupted in June or July by his exile to England. When he returned to Paris sometime after April 1304, he would have stepped into the current academic cycle of teaching, lecturing first on Book IV and then completing the other three books in the subsequent academic year.[11]

Within this textual body there exists a version of *Reportatio* Book I that claims to have been examined (a version *examinata)* by Scotus himself before his death. This text (called *Reportatio* IA) could represent the most reliable source for his final positions on a number of key issues.[12] Charles Balic (who headed the Scotist Commission when the publication of the critical Vatican edition began in 1950) held that this text of *Reportatio* IA is based upon the better of his two series of lectures in Paris and was being used by Scotus in the course of his own final revisions of Book I of the *Ordinatio*.

The scholarly state of affairs is simply not settled where Scotus is concerned. For the sake of clarity, I present below a brief chronological layout for Scotus's life and some of his works:

Year	Event/Works
1266?	Birth in Duns, Scotland
1279?	Entered Order of Friars Minor
March 17, 1291	Ordination to the priesthood (Oxford)
Before 1300	Begins *Lectura*, first *Sentence Commentary*
1300 (Summer)	Begins *Ordinatio*
1302	In Paris, begins *Reportatio* (third *Sentence Commentary*), first cycle
1303 (June)	Exile from Paris (to Cambridge?)
1304 (April?)	Returns to Paris, teaching continues, *Reportatio,* second cycle

1305   Incepted as Master in Paris. After this date, the
        following works: *De Primo Principio, Quodlibetal
        Questions* (1306-7), portions of *Questions on the
        Metaphysics*
1308   Cologne, death Nov. 8

Finally, I conclude this section by noting that there are several other textual pieces we have from Scotus. The first, already
mentioned, is his major metaphysical work on the existence of
God, *De Primo Principio (Treatise On God as the First Principle)*. This was a fairly late work (post 1305), and influenced by
his proof for the existence of God found in *Ordinatio* I, d. 2,
questions 1 and 3. In this *Treatise*, Scotus refers to a second
systematic work, *De Creditis (On What is Believed)*, that he intended to author, but never did. We also have a series of
Quodlibetal Questions, the recording of scholarly debates in
which he took part after he incepted as Master in 1305, and his
Questions on Aristotle's Metaphysics, basically a commentary
with questions on the metaphysics of Aristotle. This more philosophical text may have been the result of prolonged years of
reflection, with the final books written at the end of his career.
His commentary on Aristotle's *De Anima,* along with the
Theoremata,[13] complete the nearly-edited non-logical writings
on Aristotle's work. Among his edited logical works we have a
commentary on the *Isagoge* of Porphyry and the *Predicamenta.*[14]
    One of the most famous scholars of Scotus writing in English
is Allan B. Wolter, O.F.M. For many years, he has published ar-
ticles on Scotus and has edited translations of major texts, for
the purpose of expanding authentic understanding of actual
textual arguments. Wolter is currently publishing as much as
he can in English from various portions of Scotist texts. *Four
Questions on Mary*[15] contains the texts that deal with the Incarnation and Immaculate Conception (III, d. 7, 3 and III, d. 3, 1),
the maternity of Mary (III, d. 4) and the marriage of Mary and
Joseph (IV, d. 30. 2). In *John Duns Scotus: A Treatise on Act and
Potency,*[16] Wolter offers his translation (with Girard Etzkorn) of
Book IX from the *Questions on Aristotle's Metaphysics*. In addition, a complete critical translation of the entirety of the *Ques-*

tions on the Metaphysics[17] has been published as a companion
to the critical Latin edition. During his years at Mission Santa
Barbara, Wolter published his own translation of the *Lectura
II*, d. 3 teaching on individuation (the famous *haecceitas* that
Hopkins so loved) and sections from his political theory taken
from *Ordinatio* IV, 15 (*Duns Scotus Political and Economic Philosophy*).[18] The interested reader could fruitfully consult any of
these shorter translations with commentary to get a better sense
of how Scotus works his way through a question. Finally, *Duns
Scotus: Mary's Architect* (with Blaine O'Neill)[19] offers an excellent and concise introduction to Scotus's overall philosophical
and theological vision, providing far more historical detail and
discussion than is possible here.

THE INTELLECTUAL REVOLUTION
OF THE THIRTEENTH CENTURY

Political events were not the only excitement in Scotus's academic life. The thirteenth century was a turning point intellec-
tually with the arrival of Aristotle and Aristotelian texts into
the very young university system. While Aristotle's *Organon*
(his logical texts) had been part of early medieval culture from
the sixth century (Boethius had translated them directly from
Greek into Latin), Aristotle's *Physics, Metaphysics, De Anima*
(Psychology) and *Nicomachean Ethics* only entered on the scene
in the middle of the twelfth century.

In the American classic *Inherit the Wind* the infamous Scopes
trial is depicted in all its emotional drama. This trial involved
the teaching of evolution in a high school science class. The reaction of the fundamentalist Christian community was trau-
matic for the town and the nation. The drama brings forth the
major elements of the debate between evolution and creation-
ism in the early twentieth century. What happened in the thirteenth century with the entrance of Aristotelian thought has
something of an analogy with this more contemporary event.
While the reaction of the religious establishment was not in
itself fundamentalist, some members did view the work of the
Greek philosopher as dangerous to its moral authority. Aristotle

brought a new way of understanding and explaining reality, independent of any obvious religious tradition, and with a fully developed theory on scientific truth and the canons for a well-founded scientific argument (in his *Posterior Analytics*). In his *Nicomachean Ethics,* he offers a theory of human happiness that dispenses with any religious tradition. Without serious adjustment, his approach appeared to reduce human life to a one-dimensional, humanist world. Aristotle's pagan perspective troubled religious thinkers who were committed to a more Augustinian and Platonic vision, complete with its description of human transcendence, life after death and implications for a spiritual and moral horizon. Bonaventure, for example, found Aristotle's non-religious approach quite dangerous. While Aquinas, for his part, attempted to reconcile Aristotle's conclusions with the Christian perspective, he was soundly criticized during his lifetime and condemned after his death for doing so.

The history of the transmission of Aristotle from Greece to Europe is a book in itself. When the Library of Athens was closed in 529 by the Emperor Justinian, the texts of Plato and Aristotle, along with other pagan philosophers, went East. The Syrian Christians saved them from destruction and passed them on to their Islamic neighbors. By the ninth century, the Court of the Caliph of Baghdad was the center of intellectual life for the Middle East. As Islam spread across North Africa and into Spain, the philosophical tradition of Aristotle went with it. By the eleventh and twelfth centuries, the great luminaries of Spain, Ibn Rushd (known to the Latin world as Averroes) and Moses Maimonides were offering the most sophisticated reflection on the original philosophical texts. These Moslem and Jewish thinkers were the interpreters through whose eyes the scholars of Europe read Aristotle.

Latin scholars (that is, those whose language was Latin) neither encountered the Aristotelian corpus as a whole work (that is, in one piece) nor did the texts enter the Latin culture on their own. Texts were transmitted in sections at a time (as if in periodical installments) from the Toledo translators who, for their part, worked as quickly as they could with what they received. This received textual legacy included not merely the primary texts of Aristotle, but commentaries on his texts by the important Arab philosophers, such as Ibn Sina (known to the Latin world as Avicenna) and Ibn Rushd, along with earlier Christian Neoplatonist commentators, such as Eustratius. While the Latins knew they were seeing commentaries with the original texts, it was not at all clear to them what belonged to Aristotle's original intent and what had been transformed by the work of a commentator. And, to make matters worse, some texts falsely appeared under the name of Aristotle. The *Liber de Causis* is merely one, albeit the most famous, example of a spurious text that had enormous impact on how the Philosopher (Aristotle) was understood.

Latin scholars reacted positively to the texts as they came from Spain. Their major interest was both to understand the naturalist scientific method from the Greek philosopher and to sort out the implications of these very dense works. This work of sorting, digesting and understanding the implications of this "new way of seeing the world" was both stimulating and chaotic for the entire thirteenth century. The important political connection between the Church and the growing universities made such intellectual novelty a focal point for ecclesiastical authority in the great centers of learning, most notably Paris. As the thirteenth century unfolded, ecclestiastical committees were established to examine the works while scholars such as Albert the Great (who, as a pure scientist, wished only to "make Aristotle available to the Latins") studied and wrote commentaries on the works of the Philosopher.

After the mid-century, men like Bonaventure did not hesitate to critique and condemn some of Aristotle's conclusions on the basis of their denial of truths affirmed by faith. Because Aristotle was not Plato, Bonaventure did not approve of the way he approached questions.[20] Aristotle was too focused on the natural sphere; too one-dimensional. He denied the existence of Plato's Forms, absolute standards for human judgment. Since these were the basis for Augustine's divine ideas, Aristotle's approach undercut the traditional Augustinian explanation for the relationship of the world to its Creator. This opened the way to numerous errors, at least in Bonaventure's view. For example,

Aristotle affirmed the eternity of the world and thus denied creation. His scientific approach raised questions about the truth of revelation. In addition, as his thought was developed by thinkers in the Arab tradition, Aristotle was used to support the contention that the movement of heavenly bodies (planets and celestial spheres) had an effect upon the sub-lunar world. This meant that one could defend some sort of determinism, thus compromising human free will and moral responsibility. Finally, some Arab interpreters of Aristotle, such as Averroes, in an effort to defend the possibility of universal truth, denied the individual act of cognition and held that there was only one mind for all persons. This position, known as monopsychism, was commonly attributed to Aristotle in the thirteenth century and taught on his authority.

The three positions noted here: the eternity of the world, astral determinism, and monopsychism, all point to a view of reality that was strikingly non-theistic and (therefore) morally suspect. Monopsychism and astral determinism explained human behavior in such a way that moral responsibility could be reduced, if not eliminated altogether. The position in favor of the eternity of the world removed the need for any creator God, and undermined the authority of Scripture. In his series of lectures, the *Hexaëmeron* (1273), Bonaventure identified Aristotelian philosophy as the most serious form of error. He much preferred the Christian-friendly Platonic vision with its Ideal world, the creation myth in the *Timaeus* and the defense of individual knowing as recollection, in both the *Meno* and the *Phaedo*.

Throughout the thirteenth century, and because of the perceived threat of these new texts, the life at the university was peppered by several prohibitions and condemnations of Aristotle. These prohibitions meant that the texts could not be taught publicly: they could be read *privately*. Beginning in 1215, the prohibitions reached a crescendo in 1260, 1270 and particularly in 1277 when 219 propositions were listed as heretical. Clearly, nothing sells books like condemnations, and nothing made Aristotle a more popular author than the series of condemnations that followed, one upon the other, throughout the entire century.

Needless to say, by the last quarter of the thirteenth century
the Aristotelian-inspired naturalist philosophical worldview had
focused on an intellectual portrait of human excellence. Human
perfection and fulfillment was identified with Aristotle's discussion of *eudaimonia* (happiness) in the *Nicomachean Ethics*.
Today, we might liken it to an extremely optimistic version of a
Norman Vincent Peale variety: a theory of personal self-actual-
ization via meditation and the power of positive thinking. It
might even resemble a highly developed New Age approach. According to this philosophical, secular humanism, personal perfection can be achieved through speculation and personal meditation on the realm of the eternal and the timeless. Ultimate
human fulfillment would come as the fruit of each person's individual efforts at self-transcendence. In other words, this approach offered all the benefits of a religion without God (or at
least without the need for a personal God) to the educated intellectual of the thirteenth century. One could dispense with the
Bible or any revealed text as superfluous. All that mattered for
salvation was commitment to the world of ideas: the eternal
and perfect world. Each person was responsible for his own salvation and, as Boethius of Dacia is claimed to have taught: "There
is no life superior to that of the philosopher." As it has at the
close of the second millennium, this approach had enormous
appeal for the intellectual of the late-thirteenth century. Aristotle
had correctly outlined the journey toward human fulfillment: it
was intellectual transcendence, whether or not this involved any
survival after death.

Scotus's thought is best understood against the background
of this philosophical model, especially as it appeared in the propositions condemned in 1277.[21] Taken together, these propositions
offer a distinct way for human salvation that equates the life of
philosophy with that of religion. Whether or not any one scholar
actually held to the truth of all of the propositions taken together is less important than the overall impact of the portrait
given of the ideal human life. This life looks like a valid and
viable alternative to a Christian life. It has all the elements of
spiritual development: asceticism, reflection, self-knowledge,
meditation, good works. The keystone of the life is the intellect

and how knowledge defines human rationality and dignity. It is in many ways a framework that one finds in the work of Aquinas, who died before the condemnation of 1277, but some of whose propositions were included in that condemnation. While Aquinas nuanced his affirmation of the importance of the intellect with an equal emphasis on the will, he was criticized during his lifetime for his work with Aristotle and for his use of pagan philosophy to ground his own Christian vision.

Living and writing in the generation after 1277, Scotus's project was different from that of Aquinas. He was not about the study, understanding and integration of the insights of Greek philosophy into a Christian worldview. Rather, he engaged in a critical reflection upon the legacy of Greek Aristotelian thought precisely in light of the *caveats* raised by the condemnations. In response to an overly intellectualist reading of philosophical texts, Scotus presents the Christian vision of what it means to be human and to be rational. Scotus corrects the model offered by the philosophers and intellectuals of his generation: he does not see knowledge as definitive of human dignity, but ordered love. To the philosophical, intellectualist model of human nature and destiny the Franciscan offers and strengthens the Christian alternative, centered not on knowledge but on love. Consequently, his reflections give primacy to the will (as center for loving) over the intellect (locus of knowledge).[22]

Throughout his brief career, Scotus worked to put together an overtly Christian perspective on the world, the person, and salvation that could stand up to the philosophical intellectual/speculative model and, by using the best of its resources, still go beyond it. He used Aristotle and Aristotelian thought as much as possible to support and sustain his own arguments. He consistently defends a position wherein the fullest perfection of the human person as rational involves loving in the way God loves, rather than knowing in the way God knows. In this way, he could hold out to the philosophical perspective a viable alternative: one that affirmed human dignity, supported the human journey toward fulfillment, and still affirmed the need for revelation in Scripture. In other words, while through natural reason we can know that God exists, we cannot know (by natural reason alone) what God is really like. Such knowledge requires divine self-revelation in Scripture. This Scotist alternative would use the best of human reason to argue in favor of the Christian vision of the world as gift from a loving, personal God. Scotus called upon the resources of logic, science, art and religion to help build a view of the world that included the voice of the non-believer (Aristotle), and showed how the deepest aspirations of human nature are fulfilled with divine assistance and grace.

Additionally, Scotus's approach in this overall project can, in my opinion, be situated within the context of his Franciscan spirituality. It can best be approached when we take care to see how it fits into the larger framework that informed his entire life, not simply his teaching and intellectual reflection. Indeed, his membership in the Franciscan order may explain an early educational experience in Paris, as part of the *lectorate* program. This Parisian education may help us understand why Henry of Ghent is such an important background figure for Scotus's arguments. Again, as a religious, Scotus would have engaged in daily prayer and religious practices. Not only would these have immersed him in Scripture and given him access to Patristic sources in homilies and commentaries, but these practices would have influenced his manner of perceiving the world. They would have influenced, as well, his mode of approach to central philosophical questions that he held to be pivotal to a deeper religious understanding of life. In this way, in his work we encounter a "faith seeking understanding" in the manner of Anselm and Bonaventure, but stamped with his own Franciscan and intellectual approach. Scotus examines, with a relentless logic, the deeper metaphysical structure of a reality based upon love. This reality is entirely consistent with Scripture, especially the scriptural depiction of God as the God of the Exodus, the Incarnation and the Resurrection.

BETWEEN BONAVENTURE AND OCKHAM

Scotus did not just live in the last quarter of the thirteenth and the beginning years of the fourteenth century, chronologically between St. Bonaventure (a contemporary of Thomas

Aquinas) and Ockham (famed for his razor-sharp logic). He can
also be situated between them on an intellectual continuum. At
the higher end of this continuum, the theological/speculative-
mystical, we can place Bonaventure, with his deep spiritual insights and theological concerns. Bonaventure read the world
through the prism of the Trinity and interpreted every being
and event as a mirror of God.[23] At the lower end of this intellectual continuum, the logical, we might place William Ockham. I
say lower end here in no derogatory sense, but rather in the
sense that logic was always the beginning of any university
course of study, the foundation of good intellectual reflection.
For Ockham, the best philosophy is logical analysis, just as for
Bonaventure the best philosophy is theology.

For Scotus, the best philosophy is metaphysics, the study of
reality in its deepest foundations. If Bonaventure's approach
was principally theological and Ockham's principally logical,
then Scotus's approach was principally metaphysical. This does
not mean to suggest that Bonaventure was not capable of metaphysical or logical analysis, nor that Ockham had no theological nor metaphysical interests. Quite the contrary, each
Franciscan thinker was able to make use of all three. It is simply a question of preference and typical mode of approach.

Scotus was committed to metaphysics because he saw in it
the best way to approach all reality, all being, including God. As
we shall see in chapter 2, the proof for God's existence in the *De
Primo Principio* is itself a metaphysical proof that begins with
the evident existence of contingent beings. These beings are then
understood according to their metaphysical mode as *possible* in
order to conclude to the existence of a necessary being, without
which nothing could exist. Similarly, the defense of freedom in
the will (that we will see in chapter 3) begins with a metaphysical analysis of rational and irrational causes. His *formal distinction* (or, more properly, formal non-identity) is a distinction
based upon the power of human cognition as it relates to the
objective extra-mental world. It is a metaphysical distinction.

To the reader familiar with Bonaventure and his spiritual language, Scotus's texts appear dry and technical; here is certainly
no spiritual master. Indeed, Scotus writes more like a math-

ematician than a theologian. A northern European, he has none of the eloquence of the Italian confrere who taught alongside Aquinas. To the scholar familiar with Ockham and the clarity of his style, Scotus appears muddled and confused, introducing too many subtleties into an argument that could be cleared up and simplified so easily. What's more, he passes too easily from the human realm to that of the divine. Scotus readily uses insights about the divine nature to illuminate insights about the human. In addition, he moves from evidence about human choices to consider how God might look upon the choices open to him. He stands between the two worlds and takes from each what aids in his understanding of human reality. It is clear from his texts that at the time of his death he was still developing his most important insights, and his overall approach can be best understood as a work in progress with many questions still left unanswered, but whose broad strokes can be discerned.

Nonetheless, his approach is validly Franciscan, albeit of a dry variety, as I hope to show in this book. His insights fit nicely together, once one takes a step back to see how the basic Franciscan experience of the beauty and value of creation, the centrality of Christ and the primacy of Trinitarian love informs his reflection. Indeed, it was only when I realized the central spiritual insight about beauty and creation that grounds Scotus's thought that I saw how easily all his ideas converge around the theme of the aesthetic. Following this realization, I began to notice how many artistic and aesthetic images Scotus uses in his textual argumentation.

One of the most striking aspects of his thought is the way he uses musical and auditory imagery to illustrate his ideas about human goodness and divine response in texts such as that of *Ordinatio* I, 17. Here, Scotus identifies love as a spiritual decoration that embellishes the morally good act, one that adds beauty beyond the natural goodness. When he describes divine love and acceptance of this act, he refers to the divine ear that takes delight at the beautiful harmony of the music of human love and goodness. But such images are not simply used in moral discussions. In the *De Primo Principio*, at the close of the demonstration of divine existence, Scotus affirms that we can also

speak of God as infinite being. This notion of a being that is
infinite has nothing contradictory about it, he affirms. If it did,
the mind would recoil from it. Just as the ear is repulsed by
tonal discord, so the intellect, far more sensitive in its attention
to reality, would hear the contradiction as a metaphysical dis-
harmony and reject the notion of an infinite being.[24]

Scotus's Franciscan heritage is profoundly influenced by notions of beauty, goodness, love and generosity. As we shall see,
these themes recur in Scotist texts as he moves from the beauty
of the created order and its contingency to the affirmation of
the existence of a being whose goodness, love and generosity
are present to all that is. The beauty and goodness of a personal, loving Creator ground the discussion of divine freedom,
itself defined as generous liberality.

What, finally, makes Scotus so significant today? His thought
is enjoying something of a small renaissance, from postmodern
thinkers to students of philosophy of religion. There are several
aspects of his thought that interest our contemporary world.
First, his commitment to the dignity of the individual human
person as image of God touches our concern for this world and
its future. Second, his optimism about the created order connects with ecological concerns and with a desire for a renewed
anthropology. Third, the centrality of love over knowledge as
key to true rationality presents a different model for us to understand ourselves and our place in the world. Fourth, the importance of freedom as a perfection of God and of human reason
connects his thought to contemporary concerns for autonomy
and moral living.

Scotus's philosophical insights have a modern resonance: they
frame the human journey in terms of the dignity of the individual, the importance of rationality and the primacy of freedom. At the same time, the particular way in which they are
organized challenges us to reconsider our understanding of these
key elements in light of the perfection of human nature in *love*.
So, although he speaks with a voice that sounds modern, Scotus
has a vision that is prophetic to our modern concerns.[25] Individuality, rationality and freedom are all understood and presented by him as components of a much larger experience in-

volving beauty, joy and delight in love. Because this larger experience is so deeply affected by the Franciscan spiritual tradition and by Scotus's lived experience, his unique Christian framing of these important aspects of human experience offers us, as I hope to show, a vision of the person that is affirming, integrating, and transcendant.

Notes

[1] On the nature of the two educational tracks, see the fruitful study of William Courtney, "The Instructional Programme of the Mendicant Convents at Paris in the Early Fourteenth Century," *The Medieval Church: Universities, Heresy and the Religious Life (Essays in Honour of Gordon Leff)*, Biller/Dobson, eds. (The Boydell Press, 1999), 77-92. See also Bert Roest, *A History of Franciscan Education (c. 1210-1517)* (Leiden: Brill, 2000).

[2] If such an early Parisian period did indeed take place in the decade of the 1280's, it could account for the importance of Henry of Ghent's positions in Scotus's thought. The young man could easily have been present at Henry's Parisian Quodlibetal disputes. The findings of the editorial team working on the *De Anima* point to a dating of 1286-1292. A period of study in Paris during this time would account for the commentary's references to certain debates that took place there.

[3] C.K. Brampton, "Duns Scotus at Oxford, 1288-1301," *Franciscan Studies* 24 (1964): 18.

[4] Here again, this move to Paris supports Courtenay's suggestion of the importance of the *lectorate* track and, additionally, supports the possibility that Scotus had already spent some time there. In fact, historians have no record of anyone chosen for the Parisian degree who had not already proved himself in the Parisian lectorate program. Ordinarily, a man who had been in the earlier program would have gone back to his province for teaching or administrative work before being chosen to return to the prestigious center of learning. It also explains how he might have been known to the Minister General.

[5] R. Klibansky, *Commentarium de Eckardi magisterio* (Magistri Eckardi Opera Latina), vol. 13, xxx-xxxii.

[6] Allan B. Wolter identifies textual evidence that points to Cambridge rather than Oxford.

[7]He was elected on Pentecost, 1304.

[8]Probable dates here would be Advent 1306 or Lent 1307. See "Introduction" in *God and Creatures: The Quodlibetal Questions*, Alluntis/Wolter, eds. (Princeton University Press, 1975), xxvii.

[9]The critical or Vatican edition was begun in 1950, with the publication of volume 1 of the *Ordinatio*. The International Scotist Commission, then under the direction of Carlo Balic, worked to publish the *Ordinatio* first, followed by the *Lectura*. At the time of this writing, volume 8 of the Vatican edition (2001) completes *Ordinatio*, Book II, with the exception of questions 12, 15-25. *Lectura* I and II are contained in volumes 16-19. The *Reportatio* version has yet to appear in critical edition. Since 1950, a fuller and more moderate portrait of Scotus has emerged from the work of international scholars.

[10]That is, the *Lectura*, *Ordinatio* and *Reportatio* versions of each question.

[11]The four books of the *Sentences* were lectured on in one academic calendar, beginning with Book I in October, Book II in January, Book III in March and Book IV in May. In this way, returning from exile in April, 1304, Scotus would have picked up the coursework where it was, with Book IV, completing Books I-III the following terms. The organizational structure of the Sentences follows the pattern known as *exitus-reditus* (flowing forth of all from God and the return of all to God): Book I deals with questions about the divine nature, Book II with creation, Book III with the Incarnation, redemption, virtues and law, Book IV with the sacraments and final judgment.

[12]At the time of this writing, The Franciscan Institute is nearing publication of what Allan Wolter identifies as a "safe" text of the *Reportatio* IA (in two volumes), based upon several manuscripts, with an English translation (forthcoming 2003). The critical edition of this text is also currently in preparation by the Scotist team, under the direction of Timothy Noone, at Catholic University of America (forthcoming 2004-5).

[13]The *Theoremata*, basically a series of propositions (much like a geometric proof), may represent the rough sketch for the work *De Creditis*, referred to earlier. Because the actual nature of the work is unclear, it is included in the logical works of Scotus and will appear in forthcoming volume 2 of *Opera Philosophica*.

[14]The Franciscan Institute has published the critical edition of these two in volume 1 of I. Duns Scoti, *Opera Philosophica* (1999). Volume 2 (forthcoming at this writing) will contain the other logical texts. Volumes 3-4 contain the *Super Libri Metaphysicorum* (1997). The questions on

De Anima (volume 5) are forthcoming from Catholic University of America Press, 2003.

[15]St. Bonaventure, NY: The Franciscan Institute, 2000

[16]St. Bonaventure, NY: The Franciscan Institute, 2000.

[17]St. Bonaventure, NY: The Franciscan Institute, 1999.

[18]St. Bonaventure, NY: The Franciscan Institute, 2001.

[19]Quincy, IL: Franciscan Press, 1992.

[20]Bonaventure's *Collations on the Hexaemeron* expressly criticizes the Aristotelian rejection of Platonic forms (which he refers to as divine ideas).

[21]See my "The Condemnation of 1277: Another Light on Scotist Ethics," *Freiburger Zeitschrift für Philosophie und Theologie*, 37 (1990): 91-103.

[22] I develop this in greater detail in "Duns Scotus, Morality and Happiness: A Reply to Thomas Williams," *American Catholic Philosophical Quarterly*, 74 (2000): 173-195.

[23]The mirror imagery of Bonaventure is profoundly Franciscan, and appears often in Clare's writings. See especially her third letter to Agnes of Prague.

[24]I develop these ideas in greater depth in "Duns Scotus: Moral Reasoning and the Artistic Paradigm" in *Via Scoti: Methodologica ad mentem J. Duns Scoti*, Leonardo Sileo, ed., (Rome: Edizioni Antonianum, 1995), 825-837.

[25]I develop this more fully in Chapter 5.

Chapter 2

Creation

If you wanted to offer an explanation for the beauty of a rose, how would you do it? If you needed to explain to a friend why it is that a sunset or a piece of music has the power to move you so, how would you go about it? If you had the insight that, even if you were the only person in the entire universe, God would still have created it all to place before you, where would you begin?

In his complex and intricate textual arguments about creation, about human dignity and about divine liberality, Scotus celebrates the beauty of the contingent order as a gift of divine love. For the medieval mind, beauty had little to do with our contemporary understanding of a subjective judgment. While for us today beauty is often said to be in the eye of the beholder, for the medieval, beauty was seen as a formal characteristic of being. It belonged to the transcendental attributes of being, namely, unity, truth and goodness. Each of these attributes expresses something about being beyond the act of existence. Since everything that exists has its own internal principle of unity, and is both true (insofar as it is what it is) and good (insofar as it is the object of love), everything that exists has a beauty that belongs to it. This dimension of beauty belongs to the way the parts are related and ordered to one another. Indeed, the entire whole of creation, as a whole, expresses beauty that can be explained in terms of the ordering of parts to one another.[1]

To explain the unique beauty and importance of this world from an incarnational perspective, Scotus brings together three important truths: first, God's relationship to creation as loving and liberal Creator; second, the absolute and irreplaceable value of each being (*haecceitas*); and third, the enormous dignity of the created order, including human reflection and moral choice. All three truths reveal beauty, each according to its own perspective. Like musical harmony, the truths sound together in a single chord.

In the first perspective, God is the artist and creation the work of art. Reflection upon the existence of the work in its contingency reveals something about its author. The second perspective focuses on each part of the whole to reveal its delicacy. Here, the insight is that each being plays an essential role in a much larger whole, a role that no other being can play. Attention to the particular reveals the profound dignity and sanctity of all that exists. The third perspective reveals how, in our own lives, we are naturally gifted with all we need to know this world and to appreciate its dignity. Each particular act of human knowing brings us closer to the God who created all that exists and who is intimately present to us, both in reality around us and in the secret of our heart. Each act of human choice reveals our ability to imitate divine creativity in the concrete.

Each of these levels reveals an order that is contingent, that is, an order that is not necessary. At each level, a being exists that depends upon something else. At the level of the *existence* of creation, we recognize that this world might not have ever come into being at all: the existence of anything at all is contingent. At the level of each being within the created order, we recognize that each one might be *other* than it is: the identity of each thing is contingent. Finally, at the level of human action, we recognize that, in any given set of circumstances, we might act other than we do: human freedom has a basic contingency about it.

This chapter examines these three truths, these three notes, as the foundational harmonic constituents of Scotus's aesthetic view of reality. Indeed, all that exists belongs to a great performance by a master musician who hopes that someone is listening. In what follows, we move from the recognition of the Artist (God) to the consideration of the performance (creation), finally, to the act of appreciation on the part of the human mind. When we understand creation as the gift, the divine performance, we stand in awe of what has been given and acknowledge our inability to respond in kind.

THE CONTINGENT ORDER POINTS TO THE CREATOR

The most well known aspect of Franciscan spirituality appears, undoubtedly, in the *Canticle of the Creatures*: "Praised be You, my Lord, with all your creatures...."[2] Francis's insight on the centrality of divine love made manifest in and through creation as generous gift inspires the non-Christian, indeed the non-believer. This central Franciscan spiritual insight finds its metaphysical articulation throughout Scotus's texts about the created order and its relationship of dependence upon God. Let us begin, then, with the intricate metaphysical insights about contingency, showing how they offer a first path to our awareness of the liberality and generosity of divine love.

In affirming the value of creation and our relationship to it, we affirm the value of what is contingent and ephemeral. The term *contingent* refers to anything that might not exist at all or, if it exists, might be other than it currently is. A particular rose bush, for example, might be of another color; a particular bloom on that one bush might have a different size and shape. I might be taller than I am. I might not exist at all. A contingent being is dependent; it owes its existence to another. Even if such a being *were* eternal, that is, always existed, it still might depend upon another being, as an effect depends upon a cause. In this way, the entire created order and all beings in it might not have ever existed, or might have existed other than they do at this moment. Our order is a contingent order, it comes into being and passes away precisely because nothing about it requires that it exist.

Two reactions are evoked in the presence of such a realization of contingency. The first, more negative reaction would be depression. Too bad, we think, we are not as important as we thought we were; the universe does not revolve around us. We might not ever have come into being and still, life would have moved on. A second reaction is more positive. When we reflect upon the very *existence* of the contingent being, we recognize its value and the beauty of the present moment insofar as both can be understood to express the intention of the creator who brought it, freely and lovingly, into being. In other words, an artistic recognition of the value of the contingent being that actually does exist – coming from the realm that does not have to exist, or that could be other than it is – can give birth to the affirmation of the value of divine desire and creative, artistic choice.

The contingent dimension of the cosmic order is a focus for contemporary scientific reflection. Chaos theory points to both contingent boundary conditions and contingent laws as part of the fabric of reality. According to contingent boundary conditions, the laws of physics which apply to events that occur within the order of what exists cannot explain the singularity of the beginning of such an order. That is, the laws of physics cannot provide a full scientific explanation for the first moment of contingent existence for the universe as a whole. They explain what occurs within the whole, but not the existence of the whole itself. Similarly, contingent laws within the whole point to the fact of apparent arbitrary laws of cosmology for which there is no adequate explanatory theory. The theory itself, if found, would be contingent.[3] In a manner that would be in harmony with contemporary scientific theories, Scotus too affirms the radical contingency of all that is, in all its particularity. However, central to his explanation of contingency we discover a theory of divine rational freedom that explains the elusive contingent first moment as the intentional, free act of the Creator, just as the contingent work of art is the intentional, free act of the artist.

In the early years of the twentieth century, the philosopher Martin Heidegger claimed that the single most important philosophical question was "Why is there something and not nothing?" This is the question, not merely of what is possible, but of the *actuality* of what is possible or contingent. Were there no necessary cause or reason that explains *at the very least* the existence of what might not have existed, there would be no reason why anything exists. For Scotus and medieval theologians like him, the answer to Heidegger's question is quite simple: there is something, in fact, there is *this*, because God exists and freely chose to create this world, bringing it into being from among a host of other possibilities.

The divine being is the ultimate cause without which nothing at all would exist. God's existence becomes, then, logically necessary, the *sine qua non* for the existence of anything. Even if one were to postulate a chain of necessary causality in which each cause was itself a contingent or possible being, this would not explain the actual existence of the chain of causes itself, since no amount of possible beings can add up to the necessity of existence.

When Scotus takes up the question of the existence of God in his early teaching,[4] he makes use of a distinction within the logical order that Richard of St. Victor advanced in his *De Trinitate*.[5] Our affirmation of causality is not the result of direct experience, but is itself the fruit of the rational analysis of logical alternatives. Whatever is or can be a) either exists eternally or temporally and b) is either caused or uncaused. When each element is taken in terms of the other, one finds the following four alternative descriptions for being: 1) a temporal being that is caused; 2) a temporal being that is uncaused; 3) an eternal being that is caused; and 4) an eternal being that is uncaused. Of these four alternatives, only the second (the temporal being that has no cause) is abhorrent to human reasoning. In this way, causality is anticipated by human reasoning from our awareness of the patterns we notice in the the order around us. When some event occurs, we naturally assume the existence of some causes for it, even if we do not know what they are.

Scotus's first proof for God's existence in the *De Primo Principio* (*Treatise on God as First Principle*), Part III, takes advantage of this sort of logical insight into the uncaused existence of an eternal being. While he offers three proofs in this text, this first proof belongs to the order of efficient causality, insofar as the existence of reality is explainable in terms of a first cause, understood as agent or maker. The proof begins with the causal order of effects (a temporal being as caused). This order belongs to ordinary, everyday experience. We encounter a being that comes into existence: we consider it to be the effect of some cause. In Scotus's first conclusion, he recognizes something significant about this primary insight. If the actual existing being is contingent, then its act of existence had to have been possible. This mode of possibility can be validly inferred from actuality. In Scotus's argument, the being whose existence is contingent (yet actual) now becomes the focus for consideration of its possibility. The move from actuality to possibility is logically valid, since once something occurs it could not be impossible (otherwise it would not have occurred). The reverse, however, from possibility to actuality, is not valid. In other words, since I am sitting here now, it must have been possible for me to sit here now. However, the mere fact that it was possible that I sit here now is not sufficient to conclude that I am, indeed, sitting here now. Sometimes, things that are possible do not occur.

The move from the actual contingently existing being to the possibility of the contingent being is an important one for Scotus's overall argument. Indeed, it introduces the element of necessity into his reasoning, since arguments about the possible possess a level of logical necessity that arguments about the actual do not.[6] In his first conclusion he states, "If something is an effect, then it has the potential for being an effect."[7] The Latin term he uses is *effectibile*, able to be effected (or brought about) by another. In this way, his argument moves from the realm of actuality and experience to that of metaphysical conditions of possibility. The *fact* of the existence of anything reveals that such a being was possible, that is, it had (at one time) the potential to exist if conditions were sufficient. Since this being now exists, clearly the conditions were sufficient. One can now affirm the attribute of possibility to this being, enter the order of metaphysical consideration about the essential characteristics of the being, and consider the deeper, metaphysical requirements for its actual existence.

We have now entered the order of causal possibility, where there are beings that can be effects and, logically, they are related to beings that can be causes. These possible beings, then, can form a series of causal dependency upon one another, where each is causable (as it were) and capable of causing. Such a series, however, cannot as a whole justify its own coming to be. If we trace back the series of causes, we understand that it requires the existence of a first (his second conclusion) or logically necessary being at some point. This would be a being that exists *per se* (of itself) and has no cause (his third conclusion).[8]

As Scotus explains, one could imagine a causal chain, or series of possible beings, each bringing the next into existence, but this is not a sufficient explanation for the existence of the series as a series, unless the series *itself* were necessary. But, if the series *were* necessary, then how is it that each being in the series is only possible? No amount of possible beings is capable of producing a necessary being, or of adding up to a necessary being. At the initial point of the series, there must be something, some first being distinct from the series,[9] insofar as it is capable of causing but incapable of being caused, whose existence cannot be denied.

Another way of looking at this argument is the following: if we are attentive to a single moment in time, and to a single being in its contingent act of existence at this moment, we can consider the series of its causes to have a simultaneous and particular relationship to this one single effect. And, by making such causes of a particular type, such that their causal activity is simultaneous, then we do not have a horizontal causal chain, but rather a vertical (or ascending) causal chain. This chain is not like a series of dominos, but a simultaneous set of causes which all act at once to produce the single effect.[10] Scotus states that essential causes of such a sort would have three important characteristics. First, they would act simultaneously in producing one effect. Second, they too would exist in an order of dependency for their causality. And third, they would not be causes of equal sorts, for the higher order would govern the lower.[11]

Now, given this sort of metaphysical causal chain, essentially ordered, one cannot explain the existence of any contingent,

actual effect without a necessary first, which is itself not capable of being caused but is capable of causing another. At this
level of metaphysical speculation, however, this being admits of
only two possibilities: its existence is either necessary or impossible.[12] Since we already know that this is a possible cause, then
its impossibility is excluded and we are left with the conclusion
that its existence is necessary (his fifth conclusion).[13] Scotus
concludes this first argument from the order of efficiency with
the affirmation of the existence of God: the logically necessary
being and cause for all that exists. This being is the necessary
condition for the possibility of the existence of anything at all. If
such a being did not exist, then nothing at all would exist, I
would not be writing this sentence and you would not be reading it.[14]

So, at one end of the ontological spectrum (the realm of all
that is) we find the completely contingent and therefore possible being (me, for instance) and at the other end we see the
need for the completely necessary being (the divine). I understand that I am connected to this first necessary being by virtue
of my existential dependence upon it.

But this does not explain how God can be praised for the order of contingency that exists. It only explains my relationship
to God, not God's relationship to me. For this, Scotus needs to
work out precisely how to explain the move from this logically
necessary existing being to the actual existence of a contingent
order. In other words, how might we reconcile the necessary
existing first being with a contingent existing world? How can a
necessary being act in a contingent manner? How does this being relate to the contingent events of our world?

To answer the question of divine contingent action, Scotus
finds a helpful model in human moral action: persons make
choices. These choices express the rational desire of the agent.
The choices themselves, as well as the actions that result from
them, may or may not occur. Thus, human free choice belongs to
a subset of a larger order of events that are basically contingent
in nature. Now, this larger order of contingent events depends,
as an order, upon a first free (or rational) act of a first being. In
other words, from the human perspective, freedom belongs to

the order of contingency. From the divine perspective, however, the contingent order is itself a subset of a larger order of possibles. It was chosen among many as the focus for divine creative activity. In this way, the domain of contingency (that applies both to our choices and to the events of the natural order as a whole) actually mediates our understanding of the foundational freedom of God. Indeed, were the first being not just a necessary being but a personal being, with powers of knowing and loving,[15] then one could explain how, despite the necessary existence of such a being, this being does not relate to other beings in a necessary manner. Indeed, our world is contingent, it did not flow forth automatically from this first being.[16] We are dependent upon this being as the work of art depends upon the artist: we are the result of a free choice on the part of this personal being. And, since we ordinarily praise others for the choices they make, we can indeed praise God (as Francis encourages us in the Canticle) for such a choice: for the fragile yet beautiful order of contingent being.

For Scotus, then, the consideration of this deep, metaphysical foundation in the *De Primo Principio* is not merely an analytic exercise on the existence of God. It is, more importantly, the philosophical basis for his spiritual reflection upon the relationship that results from the divine desire expressed in the act of creation. Scotus understands God's free choice to create this world, the one that surrounds us, as well as every single being within it, as a single act of divine intention that involved many (possibly an infinite number of) options. And yet, our world was chosen and created. One does not have to conclude that we are "the best world possible," but one would be foolish not to see in this the enormous love and delight of the Artist for the work of art. But this is not all: God is not only the source for creation, active at a moment of artistic creativity. God also sustains all that is, across the continuum that we call time.

As to the second question, Scotus considers the relationship of divine knowledge to the created order as contingent rather than necessary.[17] God knows contingent events through the divine will, that is, grounded in love. Indeed, God knows future contingent events that result from human free choice by means of the divine will, present to the event when it occurs. In this way, as omniscient Creator, God is freely present in love to all that happens in our world. God's knowledge of this contingent order is not of a different type than God's sustaining presence.

Unlike the Deists of the Enlightenment, Scotus does not affirm the existence of a God who, like a clockmaker, put the whole machine together and then went off with better things to do. Rather, God continues in immediate present sustaining attentiveness to all that exists.[18] The actual and present existence of what exists gives testimony to the ever-present and sustaining love of God for what has been made. Scotus's approach in the *De Primo Principio,* chapter III, focuses on the present moment and the actual existence of a contingent being, so as to move in an ascending reflection upon the metaphysical requirements for this existing being. At the summit of the metaphysical reflection he identifies the first being, first in the order of eminence, efficiency and finality.

The contingent act of creative love reveals the sustaining act of creative presence. Both reveal the nature of divine freedom *ad extra,* that is, the generous expression of the divine nature. Indeed, God did not have to create in order to be God. Nothing about the divine essence required such generosity. The only thing required by the divine essence was that, if God did choose to create, God must remain God. Thus, creation carries within it the mark of the Creator, as a work of art carries the signs of the artist. By looking carefully at what God has made, we can conclude something about God. So, for instance, the breathtaking beauty of creation tells something of the beauty of the divine nature. The care and love that we witness in the natural world, in the way animals protect one another and their young expresses the nurturing, maternal love that makes up the divine. The undaunted power of a blade of grass to grow through a concrete slab illustrates the power of life itself, and suggests to us the power that divine life brings to our own.

Scotus considers the dignity of creation from the vantage point of a distinction within divine action. He understands and explains divine activity according to an internal and external division. Within the divine nature (God's action *ad intra*) everything occurs according to the necessity of divinity. This means that God as First Person cannot *not* communicate divine being to God as Second Person in love, nor that God as Third Person could fail to spirate from within that relationship. The internal divine dynamic of knowledge and love belongs to the essence of God as triune unity. God's self-love is therefore a necessary act because God is the highest good (the only necessary good) and good must be loved.

External to divine being, however, (that is, outside the Trinity) nothing occurs out of necessity. This is God's action *ad extra* and includes the act of creation.[19] God's choice to create this particular world, in all its beauty, can only be explained by the nature of God's goodness. The world is the work of art and God is the artist. One can recognize the artist in the art. What is more difficult to explain, however, is why God chose to create any world at all. If the Trinity experiences a necessary dynamic of knowledge and love that is sufficient to itself, then what need had God of any particular creature or of creation? The divine move *ad extra* was a contingent act of divine initiative, begun within God and for no other reason than that it was what God intended to do.

This was an important point for Scotus (and others like him) to insist upon. In the thirteenth century discussion of the value of the natural order, sources from Aristotelian and Arab thinkers tended to argue toward the necessity of the created world, both in its act of existence and in the relationships of causes. This world has value because it exists of necessity; indeed it could *not* not have been. This means that, for these philosophers, the divine act of creation was a necessary, not a contingent act. For them, God could *not* not have created: God's essence demanded just this sort of act (this world) by just this sort of being. So, for them, both what God created and that God created were necessary conclusions from divine identity. One could reason backwards, so to speak, from the created order to the divine nature. Simple observation was enough to provide all the information necessary to know everything about God. Accordingly, revelation (Scripture) was not necessary, unless you were not intelligent enough to follow the philosophical arguments. Both the Bible and philosophy conclude to the same affirmations about God, but they do so differently and for persons with different intellectual gifts.

Scotus did not think this was enough, especially for the Christian. If the Incarnation was indeed the manifestation of divine and human nature, then there must be something about God and divine action that escapes human reflection. The basic *kerygma*, Jesus is Lord, must hold some truth that lies beyond human wisdom. Human reason is able to grasp what it means, but no human would ever have entertained the idea that the best thing for God to do was to become human. Indeed, Scripture reveals something essential about God that no philosopher could have come to on his own. The divine nature as triune communion and the Incarnation as fullest manifestation of divine essence go far beyond the ken of human natural reason, left to its own devices. In addition, the *downward mobility* (Phil. 2) of the divine act of self-revelation and self-gift goes against everything that human reason accepts as *reasonable divine* behavior. In what Scripture reveals, then, we learn things about divine nature and divine action in human history. Scotus focuses on the God who took initiative in human history and continues to take initiative, and for reasons that may surpass human understanding, but are not in themselves incoherent. Indeed, there is a type of human activity that parallels this sort of behavior: the activity characteristic of love and generosity.

From this vantage point, then, creation's two-fold contingency points toward beauty and love. The existence of anything at all (rather than nothing) reveals the contingent order precisely as *gift*. At the first moment of anything at all, existence is explained as the result of a contingent act. This contingent act is ultimately, for Scotus, understood in terms of God's loving choices. But this is not all, for once we recognize that any existence is undeserved, we marvel that, out of all the beings that could have been created by such a generous initiative, *we* were personally chosen and brought into being. Indeed, contingency is not only there at the outset, but it permeates the created order down to the slightest detail. And, if contingency is reducible to love, then for Scotus, love is both there at the outset and permeates the created order down to the slightest detail. It is a lottery beyond our imaginative capacity – and, we have won! If we were stunned by the act of existence, we are overwhelmed and deeply humbled by *our* personal act of existence, and by the act of existence of our world, our universe, understood precisely as gift of a loving Creator.

DIVINE FREEDOM AND CREATIVITY

Scotus speaks of the act of creation in Pauline terms. "To make his glory known"[20] is a frequent refrain that explains divine intention in the act of creation. God chose to share divine goodness, to create *co-lovers* of divine infinite goodness and beauty. Here we have gone beyond the mere contingent order of creation and its metaphysical relationship to the Creator. To speak of the divine intention and choice is to make the act of creation not simply a contingent act but, more importantly, a *free* act. To say creation is contingent means that it might not have existed, but in fact it does. To say creation is a free act means far more. It means that what exists was chosen for a purpose and set within an intentional order. The philosophical categories we saw earlier, those of contingency and necessity of causes, along with the distinction of logically possible and necessary beings, have provided Scotus with a well-formed conceptual lens through which he views the value of each creature and by means of which he understands clearly how any contingent value cannot be the result of chance, but must come from the freedom that is a perfection in God.

Scotus explains divine freedom relative to the created order in his *Ordinatio* I, distinction 44,[21] where he uses the medieval distinction of divine activity *de potentia ordinata* and *de potentia absoluta*. This distinction within divine power explains divine intentionality and clarifies how free acts are more than merely contingent acts.

The term *de potentia absoluta* refers to God's unrestricted and absolute power, that is, all that lies within God's power to do. Because God is rational, this power is also rational and, thus, expresses the rationality inherent in the principle of non-contradiction. This principle is the foundation for logic and the rational grasp of the difference between a true and false statement. It states simply that something cannot "be" and "not be" at the same time and in the same respect. One cannot affirm and deny the same proposition at the same time and in the same way. A statement cannot be both true and false at the same time and in the same respect. A statement could be true at one time (such as "I am sitting down") and false at another (when I am no longer sitting down). Or a statement could be true in one respect (she is tall compared to her sister) and not true in another (she is not tall compared to the Empire State Building).

Since this logical principle is the foundation for rationality, it is also a characteristic of divine activity. This means that God does nothing contradictory or irrational. He could not, for instance, hate himself. He could not create a non-rational human being, since *human* means "rational animal." He could not create an angel with a material body, since angels are, by definition, immaterial beings. He could not will that someone hate the good, nor could he will that someone love evil. He could not make a square circle either. However, the fact that divine activity expresses rationality does not limit God's power. Indeed, were God to do such things, God would not be God. Such irrational acts lack perfection. Since God is God, every act of divine nature is perfect and perfectly rational. So, unfortunately for those who like to believe that God's omnipotence means that God can do absolutely anything at all, this is not so. God cannot make a stone that is beyond the divine ability to lift it! If the true meaning of power means being able to do what you intend, rather than just anything at all, then God is omnipotent because no divine intention is left unfulfilled. There are some things God has no intention of doing, such as acting in an irrational manner.

But let us return to the discussion. God's absolute power extends rationally to all possible worlds and beings in any world whatsoever. So, *de potentia absoluta*, God could create as many universes as he wanted and as many sorts of strange and wonderful (logically possible) beings. This power is so perfect in God that it can also be exercised *synchronically*. This means that at

any given moment God's freedom is equal to create a given being, and the fact that the being is created does not restrict God's
freedom *at that same moment* not to create the being. This is an
extremely radical way for Scotus to emphasize the value of anything that exists at the moment it exists. It also means that
nothing outside of God in any way restricts God's ability to act:
one divine choice does not limit or narrow possibilities as far as
divine freedom is concerned.

Once God chooses, however, *potentia absoluta* gives way to
his *potentia ordinata*. This ordained power refers not to what
God could or would do, but to what God has chosen to do or has
in fact done. Once God has set up a given created order, whatever it might be, that created order has its own internal constraints that God respects. The internal constraints of a given
order are, quite simply, the way things are there. They would
consist of the nature of beings within a world and the various
relationships among various beings within that order. An example of a constraint of our created order would be gravity.
Objects fall to the ground when dropped. They fall at a given
rate and speed. This is just the way things are here on earth.
They do not fall the same way on the moon, for example. Another example of a constraint of the present order involves the
way the human mind works, the way sense experience gives
way to ideas and ideas give way to understanding. There is a
particular way the human mind uses mental images and tries
to visualize a situation in order to understand it. Clearly, we
could conceive (without contradiction) of the possibility of knowing in a way that does not require such visualization, even though
that is not part of our ordinary experience. There might be other
beings (for example, angelic beings) in our universe whose mode
of cognition differs from ours. But the point here is that God, in
dealing with our world the way he has created it, respects the
requirements of this world as they express his creative intention.

To affirm that God respects the internal constraints of the
created order is really to say that God remains faithful to personal purposes and intentions. God doesn't go back on his word,
nor could there be a contradiction in divine behavior. Once a

divine decision has been made, it works toward fulfillment. Subsequent divine choices are consistent with this original intent. God remains internally consistent and does not waver from what he intends. Revelation in Scripture is the best account of the single divine intention of love and salvation, renewed again and again, despite human response and ingratitude. The human heart can be faithless; the divine heart is ever faithful. While nothing outside of God affects or determines divine activity, God is capable of choice that is self-limiting in its consequences and remains faithful to the original creative intention. Divine free choice is the ordained power of God as it acts in a perfect manner *ad extra* and takes initiative, intentionally seeking the divine end. In God, rationality and freedom define one another. As a creative artist, then, God is the best there is. Every work of art is a masterpiece.

HAECCEITAS

A second aspect revealed by the importance of the contingency of the created order relates more to the dignity of the creature than to the freedom of the Creator. This is seen in the Scotist affirmation of the primacy of each individual. Here is that *haecceitas*,[22] the "thisness" so dear to the Jesuit poet Gerard Manley Hopkins. Scotus explains that for any individual, the principle of individuation (what makes that particular individual *that* one and not another) must be intrinsic, unique and proper to the being itself. It must be a positive entity, a *this* rather than a *not-that*.[23] It must be incapable of reproduction or cloning: the undivided individual of each being. It can only be known by direct acquaintance, not from any consideration of common nature. *Haecceitas* makes a singular what it is and sets it off from other things like it (or of the same nature) to which it might be compared (because of the common nature). It "contracts the indifference of the specific nature to just one unique individual."[24]

Let us consider for a moment what this term might refer to and how we might better understand the dignity of the created order as the result of divine creativity. By means of *haecceitas* Scotus introduces a metaphysical principle that is not tied to

Platonic ideas or forms. My identity is not a "spiritual oneness" with others. Communion with another person, even with God, is not the absorption of my "self" into that of another, nor is it the fusion of two into one. There is no "transcendent self" to which all humans belong. There is no "higher consciousness" that absorbs me into it. My spiritual self is mine and mine alone. I shall never lose it, even in communion with God, because to lose it would mean that I cease to exist. What I share with others is my humanity and my rationality, *not* my identity. Human and rational, then, refer to our "common nature" – what we hold in common with one another. My individuality is a unique contraction of that nature into my self. I am a unique and contingent representative of the group called "human" – I possess all the relevant characteristics of that group in a "once-in-eternity" model.

The individual can be described as the contraction of a common nature into a "this" (*haec*) that is unrepeatable. Both common nature and *haec* refer to metaphysical constituents of individuality that we encounter when we meet an individual. The common nature is human nature, but this does not exist in isolation or independently of people who actually exist. We know the nature common to humans by knowing humans. In knowing several or many humans we recognize qualities, properties and characteristics that belong to all and therefore make up the reality to which the term "common (human) nature" refers. We know someone is human because he or she exhibits these characteristics. But we can never identify, exhaust, define or list the qualities, properties and characteristics that make up a particular individual, because these are one of a kind in that person. The analogy would be to a class of which there was only one member. The *haec* of anyone is, then, a sacred mystery known to God alone.

In addition to his rejection of the Platonic position, Scotus also rejects the Aristotelian explanation of personal identity. My personal identity is not reducible to my physical make-up nor to my present embodied existence. For the Aristotelian hylomorphic perspective, independent beings that exist (or substances) are composites of form and matter. The matter (or in the case of a human, the body) individuates the form (the soul) and sets it apart from others of similar kind. An Aristotelian would argue that the individual is the composite of matter and form (or body and soul) in a particular manner. It is not the form, but the matter that individuates. This means that it is not the soul but the body that defines individuality. The soul provides the formal characteristics of rationality and the body provides the particularity needed for the individual. For the Aristotelian perspective, this particular composite of matter and form, existing before us (this individual taken as a whole) makes this person who he or she is, because this person is not that person.

Scotus finds this solution unsatisfying insofar as it offers nothing formally definitive of the individual, and leaves the power of individuality to the material dimension. So, he goes beyond Aristotle when he claims that there is a formal principle (*haecceitas*) that individuates. *Haecceitas* is not corporeal, nor is it a physical reality or a composite. According to Scotus, no human person is completely reducible to physical characteristics, genetic makeup or DNA. Indeed, cloning could never replicate the person; it could only replicate the physical characteristics that belong to the person. The unique identity of each person, what makes them who they are, cannot be duplicated. There is only one of each one.

Scotus does not limit *haecceitas* to human persons. Every single creature possesses a personal *haec* that belongs to no one else. We see and appreciate this most clearly in the beauty of nature. As created by God, each being is a this, a *haec*, a unique being incapable of cloning or repetition. Each tree, each rose, each leaf knows no twin. *Haecceitas* refers to the ultimate reality of any being,[25] known fully to God alone. This would explain, he might say, why no two snowflakes are identical.

Haecceitas points to the ineffable within each being. The sacredness of each person, indeed of each being is philosophically expressed in this Latin term. According to Scotus, the created order is not best understood as a transparent medium through which divine light shines (as Aquinas taught), but is itself endowed with an inner light that shines forth from within. The difference between these two great scholastics can be compared to the difference between a window (Aquinas) and a lamp (Scotus). Both give light, but the source of light for Scotus has already been given to the being by the creator. Each being within the created order already possesses an immanent dignity; it is already gifted by the loving Creator with a sanctity beyond our ability to understand.

SCOTUS'S MODERATE REALISM

So much for reality and its relationship to a loving Creator. The Artist has performed: here is the work of art. Now, what about the audience? How can Scotus best explain what would be required for a human response? In this too he affirms the value and intrinsic dignity of the natural order, and specifically of rational human nature. By knowing the gift, we can appreciate both the gift and the giver. By knowing something about the work of art, we can appreciate the talented artist.

Scotus deals with this aspect of the created order in his theory of human knowing and its relationship of presence to what exists. In technical, philosophical terms, he ranks among the *moderate realists,* those who affirm that our concepts do have a type of real existence. This type of existence can be called *isomorphic,* or lying in a map-like relationship to the world that exists outside the mind. Thus, reality is not completely reducible to our concepts, nor are our concepts mental fictions. The conceptual order is the bridge that links our acts of knowing to the world around us, and, in this way, grounds our scientific knowledge on something actual.

This *isomorphism* is, of course, the result of divine creativity. Both the faculties of human reason and the ordered whole of creation are the result of the single, divine creative act. What is and what can be known mutually define one another. For this reason, whenever Scotus discusses reality he always refers to human cognition, just as when he discusses human cognition he does so by means of what is known. The isomorphism between the mind and reality (or between knowing and being) is essential to Scotist thought and explains how the mind is able to move from awareness of the concrete particular of which *haecceitas* is the individuating principle to a more scientific awareness of the deeper relationship that exists among natures (or kinds of things) in reality. It is also, he argues, required for the existence of any scientific reflection, particularly the more abstract sciences such as metaphysics.

This deeper relationship that the mind can recognize in things is founded upon being (*ens*), as the first object of human knowing. The human mind approaches reality with a common, basic conceptual receptivity that is open to and capable of containing within it virtually everything we can say about reality and common to all that is.[26] In other words, there is a dimension to reality that the human mind can know, a commonality (the *ens commune*) that is understood in all that exists. This dimension is the object of our acts of awareness: its unity is a common, basic foundation that Scotus calls "the not-nothing." Without this foundation, there would be neither language nor scientific understanding. Anything we can know, anything we can say about reality depends upon such a common foundation for our concepts. Not only does reality (all that exists) form such a whole, it also admits of an order. In other words, the community of all that exists is not a community of equals. Indeed, there is an objective ordering of everything, each according to its nature. Scotus refers to this as the foundational, *essential* order or the *ordering of essences*. The objective relational ordering within which every being can be considered is that of priority or posteriority. Every being (save one) is prior and posterior to other beings. The essential order joins all beings to one another and, ultimately, to God as First Principle. For Scotus, God is that Being prior to all others and posterior to none. Indeed, God does not exist outside the relational ordering, as if only the effects were ordered and the cause lay outside the relationship. Scotus makes very clear when he states, "I understand it [the essential order] in its common meaning as a relation which can be affirmed equally of the prior [Creator] and posterior [creature] in regard to each other."[27] This insight about the essential order enables Scotus to set up his proof for the existence of God that we saw earlier. In addition to the essential order, human language reflects the relationship within being, a relationship that grounds the encounter between the mind and the world. Accordingly, the possibility of language requires such a conceptual basis upon which to stand. This important basis also belongs to the common concept, *being*. This concept refers to the foundation between the mind and reality and reveals the way we come to know and understand the world around us, ourselves and God. It is therefore a *univocal* concept, common to all objects that can be known, whether natural or divine. We might understand this *conceptual univocity of being* as Scotus's version of the mind's road to God. It represents the manner of mutual presence between all that exists and our ability to know it. It is the link between our knowledge of the world, ourselves, and God. It does not reduce God to the world nor to the modalities of human knowing, but it does affirm that, in our manner of cognitional approach to all that exists (including God) we always proceed in the same manner: by means of being.[28]

The univocity of the concept *being* is essential for the existence of any science of metaphysics and, more importantly for Scotus, any language about God. This means that, if the concept that grounds natural human knowing were not a common concept that functions as basis for our language about the world and about God, then Theology could make no claim to scientific status.[29] Moreover, even in our private lives we could not say anything meaningful about God, because our language would inevitably fall very far short of our intent.[30] Theology would not offer a formal, structured way to reflect upon and express our immediate experience. There could only be mysticism and silence. Language about God based upon everyday human experience as well as conceptual reflection on revelation serves an important, common purpose in human life, even though the nature of God transcends the human ability to understand.

This foundational insight about the concept *being* might be re-phrased in the following manner: We do reflect upon our experience and we do speak with one another about our experiences of God. This is evidence that we (as rational beings) see language as a way to understand our world. We want to understand the deepest meaning of life and continually seek to express our experience in clearer and clearer ways. Now, *if* there were no metaphysical link that joined us to the divine, *if* our language actually betrayed our deepest spiritual desire, *then* the created order would be an enormous joke and our efforts absurd. This absurdity would not merely lie at the level of spiritual aspirations; it would extend to our own awareness and understanding of ourselves and the meaning of our own lives. Language would not be an aid in our understanding; it would inhibit us. There would be neither science nor religion. We would be better off as plants.

Obviously, Scotus does not think we would be better off as plants. The centrality of being as first object and the univocity of the concept *being* offer the simple explanation for the relationship between human knowing and all that exists. Because there does indeed exist this relationship of all that is and because human language (and therefore human rationality) can speak it, we have confidence in our own ability to survive in this world and, more importantly, to understand something about what surrounds us. All that is forms a unified whole that reveals the rationality, freedom and creativity of God.

Here are the signposts for the human journey: the order of beings in relationship and the importance of language to reveal the rationality of that relationship. There remains only one aspect to complete this whole: the activity of human knowing. This, too, reveals the enormous commitment to human dignity present in Scotist thought. It also reveals his Christocentric vision, since it is the person who is the summit of perfection, and not the species. Scotus bases his reflection on human knowing on the powers of cognition enjoyed by Jesus and, what's more, does not hesitate to allow for us every human perfection Jesus knew.

Scotus expands the traditional, thirteenth century discussion of cognition to include two acts: abstraction and intuition. While abstraction is more common, intuition is more perfect. Abstraction makes use of the senses and of our ordinary experience of the world around us through vision, smell, touch, taste, and hearing. The information gained through our bodily senses is transferred to the imagination which works to provide a representational image for the mind. In the act of abstraction, the intellect and this image give birth to the higher order concept for understanding. This understanding then is revealed in judgments expressed in language. Every act of abstraction involves such a *mental species* or *phantasm* (a mental picture) that mediates or serves as a bridge by which the mind can understand reality. The phantasm is also important for the birth of the concept for understanding. So, for example, when I learned to identify a dog as a dog, I did so by the accumulation of experiences of different dogs. These experiences produced in me my own "mental picture dog" that I then used as a model so that I could accurately pick out a dog from a series of several animals. This "mental dog" is a *species* or mental picture that I use to make sense of reality.

Theories of cognition in the thirteenth century made use of this "picture" model to understand how the human mind works. Precedent was found in Aristotle's *De Anima* (On the Soul) and in the writings of Arab philosophers. This model, additionally, pointed to the important role played by the body and the senses in the way the human mind (an incorporeal substance) knows the corporeal world around it by means of sense-experience. Augustine's earlier discussion of the mind in the *De Trinitate* explained how important an awareness of this representational mode of cognition really is. Indeed, once we are aware of the importance of these pictures for our knowledge of sense reality, our mind can conceive of an act of self-presence that is immediate (rather than mediated by images). By a kind of negation or removal of those images it presents to itself, the mind could experience a simple act of presence to itself. This act of self-presence is completely simple and uncluttered. It is important to note here that, for Augustine, while this immediate experience is internal and subjective, images of the mind were first posited and later removed. So for Scotus's key Christian and Arab predecessors, all knowing required the use of such images for any human understanding of reality.

Scotus accepts this model of abstraction as one activity of human cognition. He balances in his theory of knowledge both mediated or representational access with a more direct, immediate access to the world. In addition to the act of abstraction that makes uses of mental *species*, the mind is also capable of an act he calls *intuition*, where the mind has immediate awareness of the object, with no representation or phantasm needed. This act of intuition may be hampered (in our present state) due to original sin, but it belongs to the human mind by nature. Intuition is an immediate act, accompanied by *certainty* of the existence of the object. Scotus explains, "I may speak briefly, I call knowledge of the quiddity [essence] itself *abstractive* . . . [and] that of a thing according to its actual existence or of a thing present in its existence I call *intuitive intellection*."[31] Intuition is a direct vision (*visio*) of an actually existing object as existing. In Quodlibet 14, the Franciscan notes that intuition is possible due to the presence of the object "in all its proper intelligibility" and not at all because of a mental representation or picture. In the *De Primo Principio,* he affirms the superiority of intuition over abstraction because of its immediacy and independence from sense experience.

Scotus's affirmation of the act of intuition both reaffirms the link to reality (seen earlier in the univocity of being) and reveals his commitment to human dignity as created by God. First, his presentation and discussion of intuition is in light of the requirements for the beatific vision. If we are to see God face to face, then the natural capacity for this requires a cognitional theory that *already* equips human reason with all that it needs. The beatific vision is not an act of abstraction, whereby the human mind knows God by means of some mental representation or image. In that ultimate vision, the human mind and God are present to one another, directly and immediately. As Scotus works out his explanation for this more immediate ability, he offers two reasons, both based upon the dignity of the human. In the first place, such an act was part of Christ's rational grasp of the world around him and of the presence of his Father. In his humanity, Jesus mirrors our own human potential. In the second place, such a capacity is absolutely necessary for our experience of the beatific vision. In other words, if we are able to see God face to face, then our rational constitution must have what it takes to enjoy this experience, and by nature. Scotus sees no need for the "light of glory" that Aquinas provides,[32] in order for the beatific vision to take place. Intrinsic to human dignity, as currently created by God, is the ability to enjoy the relationship of communion that awaits us at the end of life.

But a second reason also informs Scotus's expansion of the cognitive powers of human nature. All philosophers who made use of the abstractive model affirmed that the senses and the body had immediate (and therefore a type of intuitive) access to the world around them. They all held that abstraction (in order to be grounded in the real) depends upon this sense-based connection to the material order. Scotus simply points out that this was an odd way of giving an inferior faculty a superior act. If the eye is capable of an intuitive act, why would one deny such perfection to the intellect, a vastly superior faculty? If the eye could do it, so could the mind.

Thus, in addition to the abstractive knowledge that Aquinas and other scholastics knew and readily used, Scotus adds that human reason possesses intuitive cognition of the world. This immediate cognition is not what we mean by "intuition," but points to an immediate existential grasp of any existing reality in its existence. Certainly, our ability to enjoy all aspects of our rational constitution has been limited by the consequences of original sin, but this does not mean such rational powers do not belong to us by nature.[33]

In this way, Scotus argues, a theologian would have a better understanding of human cognition and its potential than would a philosopher. The latter only knows what he actually experiences in the act of understanding. This is the normal act that follows mental phantasm and judgment based upon representational knowing. The philosopher would have no reason at all to imagine that another, more direct activity exists. Thinking that the present state or condition is, in fact, natural to the person, the philosopher would only assume that knowledge involves abstraction and that the object of knowing is the essence of an object.[34] Philosophers can be forgiven for their limited understanding of human potential, since they have only their present experience to depend upon. They do not know, as do the theologians, that the present state (our *status iste*) is not natural to us, but is the result of the Fall. What we experience of the world is conditioned by the results of original sin and is merely our present condition or status, not our true nature. The revelation of the Fall and consequent human weakness does not demonstrate, but gives at least reason to admit the possibility of other, more noble acts of cognition (such as intuition) that belong to us naturally. These acts are hindered in our present condition, but will be fully actualized in the next world.[35]

It is important to note here that Scotus does little more than point to the possibility of an act of cognition that is more direct than abstraction and that is finalized by objects in their act of existence. This possibility exists, he states and, if we are familiar with revelation, we can grasp this possibility. If one truly believes that human nature is fallen in its present state, then one must conclude that our *natural* state involves greater perfection, even if we do not experience it here. His approach opens the possibility to an immediate intuitive act of cognition, one that would have been experienced by Jesus who in his humanity never knew the consequences of sin. This immediate act would also be the natural requirement for the vision of God in heaven. So, *if* Genesis does reveal a truth about human nature, and *if* Jesus was truly human and divine and *if* the ultimate experience of God involves direct and immediate presence in knowledge and love, then *either* we come to this final state purely by means of a supernatural grace that we experience in heaven (Aquinas's "light of glory") *or* we as humans already possess the capacity for such an activity. Scotus opts for the second explanation here, grounding it on the requirements for consistency of revelation and doctrine and, most certainly, on the dignity of human nature as created freely by God. Accordingly, our entrance into glory involves the actualization of our current natural potential, not the reception of an additional gift that makes us both worthy and capable of the face to face vision of God. As Scotus shapes Franciscan optimism, he asserts that the human person is *already* capable of such vision. This gift was given at the moment of creation. What we await is the self-revelation of God in that ultimate vision.

A final aspect of intuitive cognition is also important to Scotus. This refers to the domain of introspection and subjective self-awareness. It is essential to Scotus that the human mind provide for the awareness of a contingent, personal experience, and with some degree of certainty.[36] This type of experience would be essential to any act of repentance and conversion. Memory has such an intuitive capacity, insofar as it brings to mind actions in the past, or events at which I was present and I am certain that I was present. These sorts of mental acts are the foundation for regret for a past action.[37] But in addition, moral reflection must have an intuitive component, insofar as moral judgment needs some level of certainty about what to do.

Beyond the acts of abstractive and intuitive cognition we find, finally, the formal distinction. In Scotist thought, here is another way to express the important connection between the mind and reality outside the mind. A *formality* is an aspect of an object that has potential for consideration by the intellect. When two concepts are formally distinct, they are one in reality and two under mental consideration. Scotus holds, for example, that the persons of the Trinity are formally distinct from the divine essence. Each is divine, yet the person of the Father is not the person of the Son. Scotus also maintains that the intellect and will are formally distinct from one another, since both are faculties of the single human soul. The way the mind and reality come together for Scotus is clear in his affirmation that the mind can distinguish aspects of an object *formally*, that is, the mind can consider the same thing from two different points of view or perspectives. Philosophy might consider the ultimate principle of being according to the formality of *necessary being*. A believer would consider that same principle according to the *God of Abraham, Isaac and Jacob*. We are not talking about two separate objects, two ultimate beings. Rather, there is (by definition) only one ultimate being. This being can be understood according to different modes of conceptualization, or differing perspectives. These modes reveal the ability of the mind to distinguish formalities within objects. This ability is based upon the potentially knowable aspects of the objects.

HUMAN FREEDOM AND MORAL CHOICE

All the above aspects point to the dignity of the created order and the enormous value of the human. This means that when we as rational and free persons choose in light of ultimate goodness, we imitate God's own creativity and are the dynamic image of God. Our contingent acts reveal finite beauty and freedom, in the same way that divine contingent acts reveal infinite divine beauty and freedom. We do not have the same sort of perfect, infinite and creative freedom that God enjoys. Far from it. Divine freedom is creative of value in an ultimate sense; our freedom affirms value yet only in a relative sense. Our choices are never the measure of the good; rather, they are measured by the good as established by God.

We might imagine the order of created goodness (or the many goods surrounding us) existing as a bridge between the freedom of human moral choice and the freedom of divine creative choice. The goods of this world lead us to God by virtue of their existence. They do not need to be loved by us in order to have value. They already possess the value of their existence as loved and created by God. It is up to us to recognize and affirm the value of creation by means of our choices. Our moral education involves learning to love rightly and in an orderly manner. It is not so much a matter of finding objects to love, since all that exists is worthy of love. It is rather a matter of adjusting our loving to conform to the worth of the object. We should not love objects more than persons, for example. We should not love persons as if they were our possessions. We should not love God as if he belonged to us alone. The message here is not about loving some things and not others. That would be easy. The message is about loving all that is, but according to the appropriate measure.

The key to this appropriate loving is found in setting all things in relationship to God, the ultimate good and source of all goodness. As the next chapter will show, when we love God above all things and for God alone, then the scale of value around us falls into appropriate place. We see more clearly how all beings participate in divine life and goodness. We also see how we, as created in the divine image, reflect divine perfection in our proper activity: loving rightly. Such an act of right loving requires the totality of our natural gifts, our rational and affective dimensions, our mind and heart, to fulfill our human nature and bring us to happiness.

In this way, like most medievals, Scotus notes the relationship of moral living to foundational metaphysical value. Actions such as respect for persons and truth-telling are good because the world exists in the way that it does and because human nature is created in such a way as to know the world and to be perfected by means of our interaction with it. Those actions that lack goodness (such as murder and lying) do not affirm the goodness that belongs to the created order and to the beings in it. At its core, the domain of moral reflection depends upon God because all created reality depends upon God. The objectivity of the moral order depends upon the divine will because the divine will is the source of the created order that, itself, is a book to be read by human reason and understood by the natural powers of human reflection.

CONCLUSIONS

In this chapter, we have reflected upon the way in which the created order leads to recognition of divine choice and creative freedom and to the affirmation of human dignity. Our affirmation of the passing nature of this world should not be a source for sadness, but rather for the recognition of our dignity and of the dignity of all that exists. Divine freedom to create this particular world and the beings in it grounds Scotus's Franciscan insight about the beauty of nature and the connection of all that exists.

The supreme value of the human person stands at the center of Scotus's vision of the created order. In this way, his vision is Christocentric, as he views both the Incarnation as central act of divine freedom and initiative in self-revelation and as the model for human actions. Jesus Christ stands at the center, both historically in salvation history and methodologically, as Scotus reflects on the cognition he enjoyed in his earthly life and uses it to frame his insights about the human experience of the beatific vision.

Finally, the particular value of each individual as created by God is explained in Scotus's teaching on *haecceitas*. Each aspect: creation, cognition and personal dignity reveal what is most important to Scotus: the value of this contingent order as it expresses divine love and creative freedom. Once we recognize the value of nature, of others, and of ourselves, we are called to act in *imago Christi*, as images of Christ who embodied divine love.

Notes

[1]Augustine defined beauty as the harmony of parts with the suavity of color (VI *De Musica*, 13, 38). This definition was taken up both by Pseudo-Dionysius and Bonaventure. It is central to Bonaventure's *Mind's Road to God*. In his Commentary on the *Sentences*, II, d.9, 1, 6, Bonaventure explains that beauty consists in order. Scotus's discussion of the essential order of all that exists can be understood to echo this earlier insight.

[2]Sometimes referred to as the Canticle of Brother Sun, given a dating of 1224-1225 in the *Assisi Compilation*, paragraph 83-84, where it is referred to also as "Praises of the Lord." The Canticle itself is found in *Francis of Assisi: Early Documents*, vol. 2 The Founder (Hyde Park: New City Press, 2000), 184-187.

[3]See Ian Barbour, *Religion and Science* (San Francisco: Harper 1997), 209-212.

[4]In the *Lectura* I, d.2,1, q.1-2, n.41 (Vatican 16: 126).

[5]Richard of St. Victor, *De Trinitate* I, 8 (PL 196: 894).

[6]*De Primo Principio*, 3.6, in *John Duns Scotus: A Treatise on God as First Principle* (translated, edited and with a commentary by Allan B. Wolter, OFM (Chicago: Franciscan Herald Press, 1966), 42. All future references are to this edition. See Appendix 1, pp. 151-57.

[7]*De Primo Principio*, 3.5, (42).

[8]The second conclusion appears at 3.7 (44) and his third conclusion at 3.16 (50).

[9]*De Primo Principio* 3.13 (46).

[10]At 3.8 (44), Scotus clarifies the difference between these two sorts of causal series. The horizontal series, like dominos, would belong to an accidental (not essential) order. Such an order, like father-son-grandson takes place within a temporal continuum and could be an infinite series. The essential order is, by contrast, a series of causes understood in terms of a simultaneous causal activity, and is therefore a vertical (or ascending) series. In the act of choice, Scotus refers to knowing and choosing as belonging to two orders of essential causality that function simultaneously.

[11]See 3.11 (46).

[12]At 3.19 (52).

[13]At 3.21 (52).

[14]Following this proof from efficient causality, Scotus provides parallel proofs from final (based on the end) and eminent (based upon perfection) causality, thus bringing together Aristotelian (final) and Platonic (eminent) arguments in support of the existence of God.

[15]Scotus does this in chapter four of the *Treatise*. See conclusion four, 4.12-4.22 (80-90).

[16]This is the main point of conclusion five (chapter four): "The first being, in causing, causes contingently whatever it causes." To possess a will is to cause contingently; therefore, if the first being possesses a will (conclusion four) it causes contingently (conclusion five). See 4.23-4.26 (90-92). A proposition claiming that whatever God does is done of necessity figured among those condemned in 1277. See my "The Condemnation of 1277: Another Light on Scotist Ethics" *Freiburger Zeitschrift fürTheologie und Philosophie*, 37 (1990): 91-103.

[17]This is a significant topic for contemporary scholarly debate, since it would seem that God's knowledge is necessary, rather than contingent. The deeper issue relates to human free choice in light of divine foreknowledge. Scotus's key text on this is found in distinction 39 of Book I.

[18]Scotus argues in *De Primo Principio* 3.14 (48-50) that a continuum of cause/effect relationships (or what we might call repeatable causal patterns) requires a sustaining cause at every moment of the temporal continuum. Thus, patterns in causality point to a first, necessary sustaining cause.

[19]Scotus points out the difference between necessarily and contingently true propositions about God (in Theology) on the basis of the *ad intra / ad extra* distinction. See *Ordinatio* Prologue, Tertia Pars, n.150 (Vatican I: 101).

[20]Ephesians 1:3-10.

[21]In Vatican VI: 363-369, translated in Allan B. Wolter, *Duns Scotus on the Will and Morality* (Washington, D.C.: Catholic University of America Press, 1986), 255-261. See Appendix 1, 158-61.

[22]The Latin term only appears twice in Scotus's works, in the *Reportatio* II, distinction 3 and in his *Subtle Questions on Aristotle's Metaphysics*, VII, q.13.

[23]See his *Ordinatio* II, d.3, n.187 (Vatican VII: 483) reproduced in Frank/Wolter *Duns Scotus, Metaphysician* (West Lafayette, IN: Purdue University Press, 1995), 185. See Appendix 1, 162-63.

[24]Allan B. Wolter, "Scotus's Individuation Theory" in *The Philosophical Theology of J. Duns Scotus*, M. Adams, ed. (Cornell, NY: Cornell University Press, 1990), 90.

[25]*Ordinatio* II, d.3, n.188 (VII:484) in *Duns Scotus, Metaphysician*, 187.

[26]Ordinatio I, d.3, n.137 (III:85) in *Duns Scotus, Metaphysician*, 121.

[27]*De Primo Principio* 1.5 (2).

[28]For readers familiar with American pragmatism, C.S. Pierce refers to himself as a Scotist, particularly where this notion of a common-sense connection to reality is concerned. I understand Scotus's theory on the relationship of the mind to reality more in terms of a Piercean perspective, than in terms of the Heideggerian (conceptualist) perspective. This means that Scotus is a critical realist (in our contemporary sense of the term) rather than an idealist. See the text in Appendix 1, 164-68.

[29]See *Lectura* I, d.3, q.1-2, n.113 (XVI:266).

[30]See *Ordinatio* I, d.3, n.139 (III:87) reproduced in *Duns Scotus, Metaphysician*, 123.

[31]*Ordinatio* II, d.3, q.2, n.321 (VII:553). See excerpt from Quodl. 6 in Appendix 1, 169-71.

[32]In *Summa Theologiae* I, 12, 2.

[33]See, also, his discussion in *Quodlibet* 14, n.12.

[34]"The Philosopher, however, would say this present state is simply natural to man, having experienced no other and having no cogent reason for concluding another state exists. He perhaps would go on to claim that the adequate object of the human intellect, even by its nature as a power, is simply what he perceived to be commensurate to it at

present, [i.e., the quiddity of sensible things."] *Quodlibet* 14, n.12 taken from *God and Creatures*, Felix Alluntis and Allan B. Wolter, eds. (Princeton, NJ: Princeton University Press, 1975), 327.

[35]"This at least is what would have to be admitted by a theologian who claims our present state is not natural and that our impotence in regard to many intelligible matters represents a penal, not a natural situation, according to [Augustine] in *De Trinitate*. 'Things that are certain are revealed to your interior eyes by that light,' namely that eternal light of which he has spoken. 'What is the reason, then, why you are unable to see it with a steady gaze except indeed your infirmity; and what has brought this upon you except sin?'" *Quodlibet* 14, n.12 in *God and Creatures*, 327.

[36]In *Lectura* I, d.3, n.172-181 (XVI: 292-297), reproduced in *Duns Scotus, Metaphysician*, 125-133.

[37]This is a strong Augustinian insight that Scotus did not want to lose when he rejected the illuminationist theory of knowledge, characteristic of Augustinian thinkers such as Henry of Ghent. Scotus saves important aspects of the Augustinian theory by integrating them into the larger Aristotelian framework of representational knowing.

Chapter 3

The Covenant

I suppose it would have been enough for God to create the world as we know it and to give us natural clues to help us in our journey back to divine communion. As the preceding chapter noted, the created order in its contingent reality points to the act of divine, creative freedom. Reflection upon all that exists, in the very act of its existence, is indeed sufficient to conclude to the necessary existence of a being without whom nothing would exist. As the history of human philosophical speculation makes abundantly clear, human reason is able to affirm that a First Being exists, without knowing in all detail the nature of that Being. It might have been enough to know that such a Being does indeed exist to begin the journey, or even to complete it for that matter.

It would have been enough for us, but apparently it was not enough for God. Divine freedom chose to go further than creation. In addition to the metaphysical relationship of being that we enjoy as part of the essential order, we also know of a deeper personal relationship that God has established with us: the covenant. This covenant begun with Abram and the People of Israel has, we believe, been fulfilled in the person of Jesus Christ and the Incarnation. The covenant is an intentional act of relational initiative, taken by God as part of his loving desire, not only to make a world, but to be personally present to that world and to the creatures in it. Indeed, the ultimate divine goal, for which all has been made, is to invite us to join in the glory of divine life.

There are two acts of divine initiative, not unrelated. The first act is that of creation, where God chose to make this world with all the creatures and natural relationships within it. The second act of divine initiative flows logically from this first, at least according to Scotus. It involves, quite simply, the way that the two orders of intention and execution are related.[1] This is the order of ends and means. The order of execution (order of means) follows the order of intention (order of ends or goals): we take a first step (order of execution) because we wish to go for a walk (order of intention). We buy a loaf of bread (order of execution) because we are making dinner (order of intention). Once we know what we intend to do, we can begin lining up those actions that will lead to our goal. We then follow through on those actions as one leads to the next. Scotus understands divine intention as the extension of divine relationship to all that is, or (in the words of St. Paul) "to make His glory known." For this to happen, there must be beings to whom that glory could be made manifest. Step one: creation. If God intended to share divine life with a created order, then that sharing would go far beyond extending existence to that order. It would include the fullest dimension of divine generosity: sharing of divine life[2] that entails a personal act of self-revelation. This divine self-revelation is what scripture records. Step two: the covenant.

Salvation history is the recounting of the story of the activity of divine self-revelation and presence to individuals and to peoples who repay divine fidelity with faithlessness. Through the story we learn of that freedom which initiated the covenant. We learn that it is powerful enough to sustain the relationship even in the face of human rejection. Scripture recounts the story of divine fidelity with humankind, from creation and the flood through the initial covenant with the Patriarchs to the Exodus. With Moses the covenant takes a legal form, in the Decalogue, the ten commandments that represent those standards for human behavior that enable the social fabric to remain intact and sustain the relationship of the person to God.

Too often believers reduce the covenant to its legal prescriptions (the ten commandments) and see the divine desire according to rules for right behavior that have little to do with our own personal happiness. For them, God is the judge who is ready to catch us and punish us the minute we make a mistake. We need to be on our guard, watching out for our own transgressions and pointing out those of others. This was the mistake made by the Pharisees. It blinded them to the real message of Jesus: that the only desire God has is to be *present* with us and to share divine life with all creatures. The covenant is not primarily about the law as law, it is about relationship and unconditional commitment.

Once we realize this, the Bible ceases to act as a rulebook and begins to look like a letter: a long letter of self-disclosure wherein God reveals the true nature of divinity in faithfulness to the People of Israel and, specifically, in the person of Jesus Christ. Christ is understood as the totality of all revelation and the culmination of the longings expressed in the Prophets and Wisdom literature of the Hebrew Bible. As the Word of God, Jesus "speaks" the divine nature to human ears, translating the reality of God into a language we might understand. That language, that reality is love and mercy, self-gift and generosity, the infinite outpouring of grace and glory that is God's own internal experience. In Scripture one does not read about God, one encounters God.

Biblical texts stand as the background to many Scotist insights about God, about the covenant and, most importantly, about the Incarnation and moral living. The message of the texts can be simply put: God so loved the world he gave his only Son (Jn. 3:16). In the preceding chapter, we saw the philosophical expression of divine love and freedom in creating the world. We looked at the dignity of what is created and how human rationality is equipped with the tools needed to move from what exists here to something about the Creator. In this chapter we shall consider more carefully the second phrase of the famous Johannine line: "He gave his only Son." The Incarnation is the centerpiece to the covenant and represents for the Franciscan tradition the christological point of entry toward understanding the trinitarian nature of God.

FROM CREATION TO INCARNATION

Scotus opens his Prologue to the *De Primo Principio* (the argument for God's existence), with a prayer in which he alludes to the theophany of the burning bush and God's revelation to Moses as "I am who am."[3] It is only within the framework of divine self-revelation as *being* that human reason is able to reflect upon and conclude to the existence of an infinite being, foundation for the natural order. In this "Metaphysics of Exodus,"[4] like others before him, Scotus integrates the central tenets of the Judeo-Christian tradition with the best of philosophical speculation on the nature of existence and its rational requirements. The divine self-revelation as *being* confirms both the possibility and the importance of language about God. Since God has revealed himself as being, human reason can speak about God in an authentic manner. Indeed, as we saw earlier, were *being* not a concept that functioned univocally for our understanding of God, theology would not exist as a science.

From the perspective of the Incarnation, creation is not an independent act of divine love that was, incidentally, followed up by divine self-revelation in the covenant. Rather, the divine desire to become incarnate was part of the overall plan or order of intention. This plan required first, the act of creation and second, the creation of beings capable by nature of free response to divine initiative, beings who were themselves able to enter into a personal relationship. Such beings had to possess a nature endowed with certain characteristics—rationality, for example, which involves the capacity for understanding and free choice. Since this nature would never be of itself divine, it would never have a status adequate for relationship to the divine. Something else had to happen before the fullness of divine glory could be shared. The two natures (divine and human) must be united before such a relationship could reach its fulfillment. The Incarnation, then, is the unifying moment when, in Jesus Christ, human and divine natures are present in one person.

As we shall see in this chapter, creation was only a prelude or first step to a much fuller manifestation of divine goodness. The move from the metaphysical relationship of the essential order to the revealed relationship of covenant and Incarnation is contained within one single, intentional divine act of love. God followed through with Jesus and (as the following chapter will show) divine desire doesn't stop there.

This ordering of all things toward Christ is clear in Francis's Admonition V: "Consider, O human being, in what great excellence the Lord God has placed you, for He created and formed you to the image of His beloved Son according to the body, and to His likeness according to the Spirit."[5] Already in the act of creating our first parents, God created in the image of the incarnate Son. Within Scotus's Franciscan tradition, the person is understood as *imago Christi* as well as *imago Dei*. Christ is the pattern, the intentional blueprint for the created order. Progress in spiritual life is seen as a process of *christification* as well as *deification*.[6] Like Francis, each human person gradually becomes united with the person of Christ until that identification is complete. Our union with God is mediated through the person of Jesus Christ, whose human nature is our nature. Such an *intentional* reading of salvation history places the Incarnation prior to creation, both because creation is in the image of Christ and because creation would have been an initial step toward the historical moment of the Incarnation. In other words, long before (if we can be permitted to speak temporally of divine activity) the created order was brought into being, God had already decided to become incarnate. This world was created so that there would be a world in which to become incarnate.

This Franciscan affirmation of the primacy and centrality of Christ has important implications for Scotus's understanding of the divine motive for the Incarnation. Indeed, it allows him to present his own quite novel separation of the Incarnation from any discussion of original sin and the fall. In order to understand this, we must remember how the medievals explained the divine reason to become human. The traditional, and most famous, explanation for the Incarnation was best set forth by St. Anselm's *Cur Deus Homo?,* an explanation that was followed by most medievals, including Bonaventure and Aquinas. According to this explanation, the Incarnation was cast in terms of a response of divine justice to offset and make amends for the sin of Adam and Eve. An act of infinite disobedience such as took place in Eden can only be repaid by an act of infinite obedience. Redemption becomes the act of remitting a debt of fallenness or sin. Justice required such retribution and this required Incarnation, passion and death. Therefore, "O happy fault" (*felix culpa*) sings the Easter *Exultet*. Had it not been for Adam and Eve, Jesus would never have been born to save us. We owe our salvation to the mistake of our first parents. Thank goodness they disobeyed, for now we both have Jesus and are saved!

In his discussion of the reason for the Incarnation,[7] Scotus finds this Anselmian explanation deeply unsatisfactory, for several reasons. First, it makes no sense in terms of divine desire and intentionality. One can explain the motive for the Incarnation in terms of divine desire, not in terms of a divine reaction to a human sin. The fact of original sin is not needed to account for it. Second, it makes sin a requirement for the highest act of divine presence in our world. Indeed, according to Anselm's argument, had Adam and Eve not disobeyed, Jesus would never have been born, because humans would not have *needed* it. This conditioned act of love on God's part not only goes contrary to all that revelation tells us of divine *unconditional* love, but it also limits God's freedom to act. Divine activity would be in response to human action.

In his response to the traditional position, Scotus argues that, on the contrary, nothing outside of God either limits or necessitates divine behavior. God acts entirely out of divine perfection and generosity. God desires to manifest his goodness and show forth his glory, as Paul's canticle in Ephesians expresses. Such a manifestation would have taken place in the person of Jesus Christ whether sin was present or not. Therefore, the *debt* we owe to the Incarnation is not a debt whose basis is human sin but a debt whose basis is our very existence. Even if our human nature were sinless, we would still need Jesus Christ to mediate our ultimate union with God. The purpose of the Incarnation is not to remove something bad; it is to facilitate a higher perfection.

As he develops his argument, Scotus refers to the orders of intentionality when he states clearly, "The predestination of anyone to glory is prior by nature to the prevision of the sin or damnation of anyone."[8] God intended the glory, both of Christ and of human nature (not to mention the created order), prior to the sin of Adam. The first act of disobedience, then, would have had absolutely no determinant influence upon the divine decision to become incarnate. If it had, he points out, then it would mean that redemption took place by chance and not out of divine intent.

Finally, Scotus adds his own compassionate reason: if the Incarnation had been the result of sin, we would have reason to rejoice at the misfortune or sin of another. "No one therefore is predestined simply because God foresaw that someone would fall, lest anyone have reason to rejoice at the misfortune of another."[9] Such joy would be counter to the charity required of all Christians, indeed, of all persons of good will. It is an argument particularly informed by the Franciscan spiritual tradition. Indeed, in Admonition XI Francis exhorts his followers to be displeased by the sin of another. Admonition IX notes that the person who truly loves another is disturbed and "stung by the sin of his soul."[10] Our response to the sin of Adam and Eve should not be that of rejoicing. In charity we should be deeply troubled and disturbed by their failure to respond to God with love. For this reason as well, if we have reason to rejoice in the Incarnation, it must have its basis elsewhere than in human weakness. While Scotus's position on the Incarnation has clearly held a minority position in the years since the thirteenth century, we do know that it had a profound influence on two important later writers: St. Francis de Sales and Gerard Manley Hopkins.[11]

Scotus lives in a Christocentric universe. Sin holds no central place in his understanding of the human condition. On the contrary, it is grace and glory that are key to understanding our place in the created order. Just as Francis affirms the centrality of human dignity (in Admonition V) before he warns against the danger of appropriation of goods and its role in human sin (in Admonitions VI and VII[12]), Scotus raises the centrality of the Incarnation and its place in human dignity before he turns to consider the nature of human failing. He frames the Incarnation within the lens of divine artistic intentionality,[13] rather than as conditioned by human sinfulness. God desired to glorify human nature and did so through the Incarnation. A single person, uniting both divine and human natures, glorifies human nature from within. Jesus is truly Emmanuel (God-with-us). Divine presence is salvific in its presence alone. The Incarnation itself redeems and glorifies human nature, thereby revealing the divine desire to be with us. That presence, because it is God, heals and saves.

The Incarnation is the supreme act of divine initiative, liberality, self-revelation and presence. It reveals another dimension of God's freedom: the freedom to initiate and sustain relational presence regardless of the human response. As the next chapter will consider in greater depth, this act of initiative reveals that *firmitas* and commitment to relationship that divine love brings in its encounter with humanity.

THE PLACE OF THE BLESSED VIRGIN

One cannot speak of the Incarnation without noting the important role that Mary of Nazareth plays in Scotist thought. He is called the Marian Doctor because he set forth the argument used in defense of the Immaculate Conception. While the Immaculate Conception of Mary can be understood as a logical pre-requisite for the centrality of Christ as manifestation of God, it is often misunderstood. This dogma holds that Mary alone was, herself, conceived without original sin.[14] Her freedom of choice in responding to God's invitation was not impeded by the condition of fallenness into which the rest of us were born. As a teaching, it is often confused with the dogma of the virgin birth, celebrated on the feast of the annunciation (March 25). The *virgin birth* refers to the fact that Jesus was conceived through the power of the Holy Spirit and that Mary did not lose her virginity in giving birth to him. The Immaculate Conception is an affirmation of Mary's dignity as a human person and is therefore tied to her key role in the Incarnation and God's overall plan. It also (as noted earlier) places the Incarnation independently of the consequences of original sin.

The celebration of the sanctity of Mary knows a long history within Christianity, dating back to earliest times. In the English medieval tradition, celebration of Mary's singular place in salvation history belonged to a longstanding popular tradition. Indeed, the Council of London (1129) formally declared and extended the celebration to all provinces. This declaration was defended on the basis of her sinlessness. While all theologians held that Mary was born without sin, there was not unanimity around the moment of her sanctification. She might, for example, have been sanctified *in utero*, as Jeremiah and John the Baptist were. Most medieval theologians (Anselm, Bonaventure, Aquinas) held that her sanctification was real, and that it occurred sometime after her conception. Following the traditional position on the connection of the Incarnation to human sinfulness, the theologians argued that if she had been conceived without sin, she would not have needed redemption. When one is sinless, one has no debt that needs to be repaid. Mary alone (of all humanity) would not have been redeemed by Christ.

As Scotus reflected upon this traditional position on the nature of the Immaculate Conception, its connection to the redemption and, certainly, to the Incarnation itself, he realized that the three points are closely related. Indeed, they are like three circles which meet and whose focal point is the centrality of human sinfulness. A different perspective on all three would involve reflection upon the relationship of sin (and the flesh) to the Incarnation as a redemptive act. Just as Scotus's position on the motive for the Incarnation sought to distance it from human sinfulness, so too the discussion of the Immaculate Conception seeks to distance our understanding of redemption from human fallenness. Scotus argues in favor of a renewed anthropology in light of human nature, dignity and divine liberality. This renewed vision could then replace that based upon sinfulness, justification and divine forgiveness.

Two fundamental problems had to be addressed in order to advance the renewed, optimistic anthropology. The first required a separation of "original sin" from human concupiscence, or the desires of the flesh. It meant a rejection of the Augustinian model for sin, and especially for original sin, along with its transmission through sexual intercourse. Augustine's model explained the human condition in terms of the contraction of original sin by the physical encounter of the soul with the "infected flesh." The flesh was "infected" by the inordinate pleasure experienced by the couple in the act of intercourse. Because this pleasure was beyond what rational behavior required, it was lust, and such lust was sufficient to contaminate the matter (the body) which would receive the soul. The soul, thus contaminated, would inherit physically the condition of original sin and the punishments that go with the condition (pain, sickness, suffering, death). If original sin and concupiscence could be separated, then it is logically possible that a person be conceived in a normal, human sexual way (as Mary was) and not contract original sin.

The second problem to be addressed flowed logically from this first. If there were such a person who did not contract original sin, then in what sense would that person need to be saved? Would a sinless person not need Christ? Could one argue in such a way that this person, despite her sinlessness, was still indebted to Christ for something?

One could proceed in two ways on this. First, one could emphasize the union with God that human nature enjoys in the Incarnation, thus arguing that even sinless human nature needs Christ for this. Second, one could offer a preventive argument in favor of redemption. That is, in view of the goal of the Incarnation and the merits of Christ, Mary would be protected from contracting original sin at the moment of her conception. Then she would be sinless by the grace of God and the merits of Christ, not by her own.

As noted earlier, Scotus sees the Incarnation primarily as the act by which human nature is joined to union with God and only secondarily as the act by which human nature is freed from sin. Even if there were no need for remission of the debt of our first parents, human nature would still need the Incarnation for the ultimate goal: union with God. In this way, the argument for the Immaculate Conception actually shores up the argument about the Incarnation and divine desire to become human *independently* of human sinfulness. The Immaculate Conception is the logical next step in a Christocentric world-view.

Scotus's defense of the Immaculate Conception[15] drives a wedge between human desires (especially sexual desires), sin and redemption, understood as the repayment of a debt. It affirms the natural goodness of human desire, including sexual desire. It locates sin in the soul and not in the body. It admits the physical consequences of a fallen condition without blaming the body. Finally, it defends the complete redemptive act as meaningful *even for those not slaves to sin*. Indeed, Scotus argues, Mary's innocence requires redemption even more than does Mary Magdalene's restoration to grace. When one is preserved from sin, this is a greater gift than when one sins and is restored to wholeness. In the Immaculate Conception, Mary's debt to God and to her Son is the greatest debt of all: it is the debt of her full human dignity, unsullied by sin. This debt is repaid by human gratitude: it is the debt of love.

Let us consider more carefully how Scotus re-frames his renewed, Christocentric anthropology as it applies to Mary. As stated above, the first point of his solution involves the separation of original sin from human desire and concupiscence. The second separates the need for Christ from actual sinfulness. Both entail a rejection of the traditional Augustinian model, with its description of original sin and the transmission of sin through sexual intercourse. Scotus's first move here involves the acceptance of Anselm's position on original sin that describes it as "a privation of original justice" in the soul, not a condition associated with the body.[16] As Scotus develops this point, he understands the original state of nature (Adam and Eve prior to the Fall) as higher than nature, a preternatural state of human harmony. Baptism, as sanctifying grace, belongs to another order (not preternatural but supernatural) and restores the soul by remitting original sin. However, baptism does not restore the person to that preternatural state of the first parents. After baptism, the soul is restored, but the punishment is still present (this explains the conditions of mortality and suffering). While the body is not to blame (since only the soul can sin), it still carries the consequences that are genetically bound to the human condition and passed from one generation to the next. Grace can thus exist in the soul without restoring the preternatural gifts. If the body were the cause for original sin, then grace would not only restore the soul, but would re-constitute the preternatural condition, since the two states (remission and punishment) could not co-exist.

All this means that the *physical* condition proper to human nature post-Eden is not what is meant by the term "original sin." One can inherit the natural, *physical* condition and not inherit the sin. So there could be a person who might receive the gift bestowed in baptism (that is, sanctifying grace) without the prior loss of the original justice. This person would enjoy a *protective* act of grace in the soul (in light of sinfulness), yet still live with the bodily conditions that belong to the present, natural state. Indeed, such protective action could be taken by God relative to someone in virtue of a future role that person might play, or in virtue of the future merits of that person's son. In this way, Mary's soul was *preserved* or *protected* from slavery to sin. Yet she still needed redemption because she was conceived in a natural way and lived with the consequences of the human condition.

Since preservation from evil is a far greater act than remission of sin, God's salvific action is far greater in a case where sin is prevented than in a case where grace is restored. This means that salvation does not depend upon the presence of sin, nor is actual sinfulness a necessary condition for it. The Incarnation, once again, appears as the greatest act of divine initiative and love, independent of human fallenness. Mary did not have to have sinned in order need a savior.

While this position on the Immaculate Conception is the one Scotus favors, he does admit the possibility of another, earlier solution proposed by Henry of Ghent in 1293. Henry had sought to satisfy all parties in the dispute when he suggested that Mary's conception could have been followed instantaneously by her *sanctification* in the womb, thereby admitting both her (all too brief) sinfulness and her (near) Immaculate Conception. According to Henry's Augustinian-based approach, Mary would

have been conceived in sin, as are all humans, but then miracu-
lously sanctified at the same instant. When he presents this
solution, Scotus explains that if what Henry is trying to do is to
collapse the interval of time to its smallest fraction of a second,
then this is a solution that is tenable. And, since a single moment in time does not belong to the continuum of temporal duration, one could logically claim that "at no time did Mary have
original sin." In preferring his own solution to Henry's, Scotus
states that, even if he is wrong on the matter, he prefers to err
in excess rather than deficiency by according the greater (immaculate) glory to Mary. Following Franciscan William of Ware's
earlier methodology for this question, Scotus concludes that his
position is indeed logically possible; it is also fitting and in harmony with tradition. On this basis, one has no reason to deny
such graciousness to God or such dignity and purity to Mary.

Together, Scotus's positions on the Incarnation and the Immaculate Conception point to three central Franciscan insights:
the goodness of creation, the dignity of human nature and the
graciousness of God. All three work harmoniously to frame his
position on the relationship of God to the order created out of
divine love: both persons and nature. In this vision, it is the
abundance of grace that takes center stage, a grace that is always at work in the created order, because God's loving presence is dynamic and life-giving.

THE CENTRALITY OF RELATIONSHIP

Both in creation and salvation history, Scotus affirms the centrality of relationship as the foundation for rational living.
Scotus's emphasis on relationship in his moral discussion[17] parallels the development we have followed thus far. There is a
metaphysical foundation for moral living in creation and the
order of essences. Each being has a particular nature that is
worthy of a certain place on the scale of created beings. This
nature is set forth by God and measures the amount of love the
human heart ought to give it. Because of what each being is, it
should not be loved more than it deserves, nor should it be loved
less than it deserves. In this way, human moral living has an

objective reference in the external order of created things. It is objectively connected to the divine creative will and to the rational ordering of the natural order. Traditionally, the rational human grasp of the ordering of creation is call *natural law*. It is *natural* in two senses: it is based upon the natural order found around us and, more importantly, this order is accessible to natural human reason, without the need for any special revelation.

In addition, there is a revealed (or scriptural) foundation for moral living in the covenant, especially the covenant with Moses. This is expressed in the commands of the Decalogue (the ten commandments) and gives more precise information about how we show our love for God in loving our neighbor. While the non-believer is perfectly capable of right action by means of her native rational gifts and her ability to judge objects around her (because of natural law), the believer understands how right action not only fulfills the metaphysical requirements of reality, but also strengthens her relationship to God in love. For the believer, then, every right action possesses a double dimension: the rational judgment that affirms the rightness of the act and the affective motivation that sees beyond principle to love for God.

Let's use an example to understand this double dimension. Consider two acts of kindness, identical in every aspect but one. We'll use something very simple: helping a stranger with directions. I am walking in the neighborhood and someone drives up and stops to ask me how to find a certain street. Let's imagine, first, that I am a generous humanitarian. I do good deeds because I have a generic but deep love for humanity and I would want someone to do the same for me. I try to perform random acts of kindness whenever I can. I do not hesitate to help out and quickly assist the stranger. Nothing complicated here: a very good human action.

Now take a second variant of this example. I am still a generous person and try to do good whenever I can. The person who stops me does not know me, but I know him. He is, in fact, the brother of a good friend and colleague of mine. He is asking for directions to her house. I quickly assist the person and he drives off happily.

What is different in these two examples? Clearly, in the second, my act not only affects the happy stranger but also strengthens my friendship for my colleague. I see my action within a much larger and, indeed, more focused context than "random acts of kindness." While, to the stranger, my act appeared random, there is (in fact) nothing random about what I have done. I have both done the right thing, the thing any rational person would do in that case, and I have also done something more. I have intended to help the person and, through this act, strengthened my relationship with my friend.

For Scotus, the revelation of God's desire for us in the ten commandments does not replace human rational judgment. The Decalogue does not provide us with moral information we could not get otherwise. Scripture here gives no new content. It does, however, contextualize the content of moral living within a relational order. It focuses and intensifies those actions that express moral goodness. In other words, there is nothing objectively new revealed in the Decalogue; however there is something *subjectively* new. The commands reveal divine intent for our relationship with one another *precisely as the expression* of our relationship with God. In the words of John: how can we love the God we do not see, if we do not love the brother or sister we do see (1 John 4:20)?

This subjective and relational dimension appears in the way Scotus deals with the commands of the Decalogue in III, d. 37.[18] The ten commandments fall into two categories: those dealing with God and those dealing with the neighbor. The commands that admit of no exception are those dealing directly with God as the object of our love. Their truth is immediately evident to anyone who understands the statement: If God is God, then God is to be loved. As the highest and most perfect being and, consequently, the highest good, God deserves to be loved in an unconditional manner. This is the first commandment: I am the Lord your God, you shall have no gods before me. The second follows from this: You shall not take the Lord's name in vain. Because God is who God is, one should never use God or speak disrespectfully of God. These two commands are true not because they are revealed, but because of the meaning of the terms. It is for this reason that they hold in an absolute manner. In this way, Scotus sets forth a rational and natural foundation for the moral law revealed in Scripture.

Scotus holds that, while the third command (Keep holy the Lord's day) is reasonable in terms of the first two, the other seven (all dealing with the neighbor rather than God) do not have the same sort of foundational truth value as do the first two. Their value depends upon the first and lies in a relationship of harmony or consonance with the first. They are rational and belong to natural law: they can be understood by human reason independently of scripture, but they are not grounded in the same way the first are. They are not analytic truths, whose necessary truth is known from their terms. Rather, the force of these commands derives from the divine will which created both human nature and the means by which human nature would reach its moral fulfillment. In this way, from the human perspective all the commands of the Decalogue are requirements for our nature, and all belong to natural law. We do not have the moral authority to make exceptions to them. However, from the divine perspective they are the conditions for this particular order, as constituted by divine love. Our fulfillment of these commands introduces us into that order of love and divine intention for us.

For the believer this means that, in addition to natural reflection on human nature, God has given an additional support for moral action: the divine desire regarding human fulfillment. Because the last seven commands of the Decalogue reveal God's desire that we love one another and that through this love we fulfill the command to love God, the believer discovers the reason behind moral commands.[19] The reason that is foundational to moral living is not obligation or law, but rather love and relationship. In loving the neighbor, the believer strengthens both the relationship to the neighbor and the relationship to God. There are, therefore, only two commands: love for God and love for the neighbor. This is the whole of the law, beyond these two there is no other.

Because Scotus separates the first two commands from the last seven, he cannot be ranked among those thinkers who advance what is known as a divine command moral theory. A divine command theory states that all moral obligation ultimately derives from the fact of the divine will. While clearly the last seven commands can be seen to be based upon the divine will and intent, the first two cannot. Ordinarily, divine command theories are vulnerable to the critique that while all moral laws are reducible to the divine command, obeying the divine command cannot itself be explained in terms of divine command without creating a vicious circle. Thus, divine command theories seek to provide a foundation for moral living but cannot defend their moral foundation without begging the question. In Scotus, the foundation is identified in the essence of God as highest being and greatest good. Love for God is a self-evident moral proposition, whose truth does not need to be founded upon any other and which serves as the foundation for the rest.[20] In this way, Scotus falls within the larger voluntarist *type* of tradition (because he emphasizes the will as he does), without himself being a divine command theorist (because the first command is an analytic truth).

THE INNER WORKINGS OF THE HUMAN HEART

Moral living is also relational living within the human heart, where the two natural affections for justice and for happiness come together in the desire to love God above all things. Thus, moral goodness involves both a social dimension and an internal, spiritual experience of harmony and integration. The joy and delight experienced by the good person reveals that the deepest human longing is fulfilled by right and ordered loving. This perfects our nature as rational beings made in God's image.[21]

Scotus takes from Anselm's *De Casu Diaboli* (*On the Fall of the Devil*) the basis for his discussion of the two affections (or metaphysical desires) within the will.[22] Metaphysically (not emotionally) human desire has two natural and foundational orientations: one focusing inward, the other outward. The first, toward self-preservation and conservation, is called the *affectio commodi*, sometimes translated as the affection for possession or happiness. The best way to understand this orientation would be as the medieval version of the basic instinct for self-preservation that belongs to all living beings. In animals and humans, this natural instinct gives rise to emotional responses, such as fear, anger or the rush of adrenaline when we are in danger. We see this desire through its effects in behavior or internal psychological states. While the natural purpose of the affection is the survival of the being, in humans it does not always appear as positive. In unhealthy human behavior, for instance, it can express itself in obsessive concerns for self. Fear can become paranoia; anger can be sustained in resentment. This naturally good *affectio* can thus be disordered by our free choice. Scotus accounts for sinfulness in terms of the uncontrolled or disordered *affectio commodi*. He explains Satan's fall not in terms of pride, but in terms of disordered self-love.

The second, higher metaphysical affection is called the *affectio iustitiae* or the affection for justice or for the just. This affection has a focus beyond the self and is oriented toward goods around me and seeks to love each in accordance with its worth. The affection for the just looks beyond me, while the affection for possession looks at me. According to Scotus, the *affectio iustitiae* belongs to human nature insofar as it is rational and free: it was not lost (as Anselm held) through original sin. It is a requirement of free choice. Thus, in every rational choice both affections are present and at work. The key to right loving lies in the appropriate relationship between them. This relationship was affected by the Fall; the two moral affections are no longer in a close, harmonious working relationship.

Concerns for self always play a moral role because they are the natural foundation for life. But such concerns should never, alone, dominate choice. They are ordered and moderated by the rational concerns to do what is right. When I am honest with myself and with others, for example, I feel good about myself. If I am morally mature I do not pursue honesty merely because it makes me feel good about myself. I pursue honesty because the truth has a value independent of my own feelings about myself. Honesty is the right path for me to follow in life. This path is rational and therefore liberating. It satisfies the *affectio iustitiae*.

The only way I might know for certain that I perform an action because it is right would be to look for examples in my life where being honest cost me something, either the respect of others or some good I desired for myself. In such cases of decision, I have a clearer understanding of my own character and what motivates me.

Even though examples of hard decisions do reveal how the *affectio iustitiae* governs my behavior, it would be an error if I were to understand these two affections according to a more contemporary "selfless vs. selfish" dichotomy. This dichotomy belongs more properly to the last few centuries of moral reflection. It has taken root in religious traditions that embrace a more negative anthropology, viewing human affection as suspect. It was supported in the development of an obligational morality over the last few centuries. Scotus has both a positive anthropology and a moral theory based upon harmony, not obligation. The *affectio commodi* is not a "selfish" affection. Rather, it expresses the concern for self that is necessary for survival. Nor is the *affectio iustitiae* a "selfless" affection. I can, for example, desire to be a person of integrity. Here, my own moral goodness (my self perfection) is willed in accordance with the affection for the just (an objective moral good). This sort of choice brings both affections into ordered harmony and reveals how moral integrity is, for Scotus, the source of happiness.[23] It also shows clearly that natural perfection lies in a harmonious relationship with moral goodness.

The affection for happiness is not selfish; it is self-interested, however. But, if we remember the earlier discussion of human dignity in Chapter Two, we must have a healthy concern for our own dignity. To ignore our value diminishes God's creative act. Concerns for self must be governed and moderated by awareness of intrinsic worth and self-knowledge. While I love myself, I should not love myself as if I were God or in place of God. There are times when I should rightly and justly demand respect. This is not selfish. We know how difficult it is for victims of abuse or persons in co-dependent relationships to acknowledge and defend their own rights and dignity. Persons troubled by a false sense of guilt are loath to defend themselves from abuse.

There are two extremes that we can imagine in terms of these natural affections. The first appears in the oppressive dominance of the *affectio iustitiae* over the *affectio commodi*. Here, as mentioned above, concerns for self are denied in favor of "moral behavior" that is understood to be totally other-centered at the unhealthy expense of the self. Morality is seen as something that is both difficult and, in some cases also involves a triumph of a higher will over a lower, chaotic self. Since this approach depends upon a negative anthropology, natural desires are viewed as suspect and in need of control and, possibly, suppression. The moral choice is understood as what no one *wants* to do, but everyone *has* to do. In religious language, it is what you do "to get to heaven" or "to avoid hell." Moral living is reduced to legalism; obligational morality commands certain behaviors.

The other extreme involves the exaltation of the *affectio commodi* over the *affectio iustitiae*. This would be where what I think is right becomes objectively the good to be done. My desires are infallible because I say they are. My choices define goodness because I say they do. In an era of "I'm OK, you're OK" this is the reaction to decades of obligational morality. The self has returned today, with a vengeance!

Scotus rejects both extremes. His discussion of choice brings both affections into mutual relationship. Both are present in every human choice, because, first, my choices are mine (*affectio commodi*) and they define my character; and second, because my choices are rational and free (*affectio iustitiae*) because I am human and, therefore, rational and free. My nature as a person defines my behavior insofar as every choice I make has a personal, rational and (to some degree) free dimension. The modern or contemporary moral dichotomy between what I want and what I must do disappears in Scotus. There is no sharp division nor is there radical conflict between who I am and who I ought to be. This is due to his positive anthropology. Human nature is not suspect. Nor, however, is it perfect and complete from the outset. The affections are not properly balanced, and we must learn to bring them into greater harmony with one another. In this way, moral education and living is perfective of natural human goodness. The moral context is the place where we learn right and ordered loving. As we know, this education takes a lifetime to perfect.

THE RATIONALITY OF FREEDOM

Scotus describes human free choice most fully in terms of the two affections within the will. This means that freedom is defined as rationality and that rationality is defined as freedom. How might these two key human aspects mutually define one another? We might answer this question by looking more carefully at each one and discerning what, if possible, can be found beneath them both.

Let us first take up the idea of freedom for further consideration. Here, of course, we mean moral freedom or freedom of choice. This is the freedom of self-movement that belongs to the will alone. In one of his more philosophical works,[24] Scotus offers a key distinction that will appear much later in the history of moral reflection: the distinction between natural causes that are determined and free causes that are indetermined.[25] An example of a natural cause would be the fall of a stone. Once in motion, the falling stone cannot stop itself. It can only be stopped by some external impediment. The will is the only example of a free cause. Scotus uses the distinction among moving causes to highlight the indeterminate freedom of the rational will. It is, he states, a cause unlike any other cause. The rational will has that internal relationship to itself such that it (and it alone) is a *self-mover.* When we remember that, for Scotus, the term *will* refers to the human person insofar as she loves, desires and chooses, this self-relationship involving initiative and restraint is another way of speaking of reflective, rational desire: the foundation for moral choice.

So, what might Scotus mean when he speaks of freedom as self-movement? He might mean no more than the conscious awareness of our own desire as *our* desire. But consciousness is not enough for freedom, so there must be more than this. When, for example, I desire something without knowing what it is, my

mere consciousness of my desire is not synonymous with freedom or free choice. I can imagine myself, first, as merely aware
of a vague desire. This is quite distinct from understanding
myself as someone who is both aware of a desire and who pur-
sues the object of that desire. Here the notion of rational self-
consciousness has helped us. It defines a self-relationship that
is capable of explaining self-movement. However, we are still
missing the point of free choice: where the person shifts from
inaction to action.

What we need to find is an example where there is no object
outside the will to move the will from inactivity to activity, yet
the will moves all the same. Or perhaps we could use the opposite situation. In other words, let us take a situation where there
is nothing but objects outside the will to move it, and the will
does not move. We might imagine someone who has stopped
smoking, in a room filled with people who smoke. This person
desires to smoke, has reason to smoke, knows what he desires
and is able to get it. Yet he does not smoke. Why? Or better yet,
how?

Self-relationship explains both self-restraint and self-movement. In fact, the capacity of the will for self-movement is the
same as the capacity for self-restraint. To lose one is to lose the
other. Self-restraint is another way of talking about self-control
and the capacity of the person to have power over his own actions. We have come from the concept of freedom through that
of self-movement, to an understanding of self-restraint and self-
control.[26]

Now let's begin again from the idea of rationality and see where
that leads us. Here, I think, we can move relatively quickly from
the rational to the conscious self-awareness that we all experience. In our awareness of our desires, we note that some objects
are preferable to others. Some objects, like friendship, represent the ultimate in a certain genus, the genus of love. Those
desires are rational which lead to the higher goods, the goods
beyond measure. We act rationally when we choose those in preference to other, lesser goods, because they are worthy of our
choice. This ability to choose a higher rather than a lower good
depends upon the control we have over our own selves and our

impulses. Scotus lays out the foundation for this ability in the two affections we saw earlier. These two affections express the spectrum of all desire and, in addition, the self-relationship found within the will. When Scotus explains that every choice involves both desires, he means that in every choice the will experiences itself in an internal self-relationship grounded in its own nature as faculty of rational desire. We experience this self-relationship when reason governs choice or, in other words, when we are in command of ourselves and experience self-control. Here we have moved from the notion of the rational almost immediately to that of self-control.

So, both the reflection on freedom and the reflection on rational have led us to a reflection on self-control. Self-control, then, I suggest is that act which reveals human freedom as Scotus understands it. It is that "liberty innate to the will" that grounds moral responsibility and explains self-movement. It holds the key to the perfection of willing as rational and as free. And the perfection and fulfillment of the human person is revealed in an activity of love that is both rational and free. Scotus holds that, in the beatific vision, the human person loves God without losing her freedom not to love God. How is this possible? For Scotus the answer is quite simple. Because the person has a will composed of the two affections, those two affections define the will insofar as it is a free will. In heaven the will continues to be itself and, thus composed of the two affections, never loses its freedom. Because part of the will's freedom involves the act of self-restraint the will of the blessed in heaven might remain in God's presence and simply restrain itself from choosing God. This would be the act of *non velle* or non-choice, rather than rejection. For the will to remain responsible for its acts, even in heaven, it must retain the capacity to control its own choices. For Scotus, this means that the will remains free for the act of choice (*velle*), rejection (*nolle*) and self-restraint (*non velle*). In other words, the will continues in its natural constitution of the two affections (*iustitiae* and *commodi*) which, for their part, define it as rational. In the presence of God, the will has no reason to turn away (*nolle*) but might, conceivably "hold itself back" from the act of love. Here, divine love acts in the form of *voluntas praeveniens*, or prevenient grace to uphold, support and otherwise assist the will in its loving regard. And in the presence of such grace, it would be impossible for the will to choose not to love God. For, at that moment, to choose not to love God would be analogous to a lover having no reason to turn away from the beloved, due to the strength of the beloved's love for the lover. The lover, though able, does not choose to "hold back" because of the experience of love.

THE INTELLECT AND THE WILL GIVE BIRTH TO THE MORAL ACT

The terms *intellect* and *will* are foundational vocabulary to medieval discussions of human action. This approach is known as *faculty psychology*, because it considers the human soul according to its faculties (intellect and will). This sort of terminology is helpful for technical analyses and systematic consideration. It can, however, cause confusion, when we forget that the terms themselves have no reality outside the human person. The term *intellect* is a shorthand way to refer to the person considered as one who knows and understands. The term *will* is, likewise, a shorthand term for the person considered as one who desires, loves and chooses. Scotus is clear in his affirmation that these two faculties (intellect and will) are formally distinct from one another and from the human soul. This means that there is no time when they exist separately from one another or from the person whose intellect and will they are. When Scotus integrates the intellect and will into moral action, he attempts to integrate rational desire as a single manifestation of human perfection. When he prefers the will to the intellect, he is viewing the whole from the perspective of love and desire, rather than the perspective of knowledge and understanding.

The will's rationality, then, both refers to its ability to control itself and to the fact that it does not act alone in moral choice. The intellect aids in "bringing to birth" the moral act. Scotus uses this imagery in his *Lectura* II, 25 discussion of how the will and the intellect cooperate in acts of choice.[27] Because of his insistence on the importance of freedom for the will, Scotus subordinates the influence of knowledge to that of self-determined freedom. In fact, he maintains that a person can know with certainty (through abstraction and intuition) what the right thing to do might be, and still not do it. This is because the intellect provides the information relevant to choice to the will, and the will retains the power either to cooperate or not. In this way, Scotus understands the will to be a rational potency rather than an intellectual appetite.

So, what does this mean? It means, first, that no act of choice takes place in the absence of an object or something to be chosen. The intellect always contributes to the act of choice by presenting the object to the will. The intellect also has a double capacity for knowing: abstraction and intuition. This means that the intellect has a level of certain knowledge that it might attain. Once present to the will, however, the object known falls within its power and is now internal to it. At this point, because the will is fully self-determined, it has all it needs for choice. Without the presence of the intellect or act of cognition, Scotus maintains, the will would be blind. With it, one may speak of free will or free choice in the rational agent.

Secondly, though, it means that the will has access to a self-reflexive cognitive act, wherein it could consider itself or its own act as the object, rather than an object external to it. For example, I can know something about a choice before me (choosing dinner from a menu, for instance) that involves considerations about options (chicken or pasta), about my health concerns, about my financial situation, etc. I can also, however, consider a choice I am about to make in terms of itself, that is, as an act of right and ordered loving. So, for instance, I could consider "Should I choose rightly in every future choice?" In such a situation, the intellect is fully present to the choice as before (when I chose from the menu), but this time, the intellect is presenting me to myself, as it were. This choice is not a choice between small options, but a basic moral option for my life. In such a situation, both cognition (the intellect) and desire (the will) are functioning as a single, rational agent, producing a single, rational choice.[28]

Nothing outside the will determines its choice.[29] This means that the only determinant in choice is the will, with all that lies within it. Since, as we saw above, the will refers to the person insofar as he desires the good, this means that choice is determined by the individual insofar as he desires the good, and by nothing outside of him. Here, we might consider all that factors into a decision about a given object: past experience, traits of character, intention and motivation. All these belong to the person insofar as he desires the good; all these belong to the will as seat of love, rationality and freedom.

Historically, some scholars have considered Scotus to hold an empty, almost an arbitray notion of freedom. When he states that nothing outside the will determines its choice, this can be taken to mean that he holds to a type of pure freedom that exists independently of all rational factors, and that this freedom lies at the heart of all choice. Such freedom has no content; its essence is its exercise. This interpretation depends upon a notion of rationality that is, I would argue, more intellectualist than voluntarist.[30] In other words, if reason belongs to the intellect and if the intellect is not in the will, then when nothing determines the will other than itself, this power to choose appears to have a freedom that is, quite simply, irrational. Where Scotus is concerned, however, this is far from the case. The Franciscan affirms, time and again, that the will is the sole rational potency. For him, when nothing other than the will determines its act, then the will is in its own power and that power is moral rationality: self-control and self-determination, according to the light of reflection.

MORAL AND NATURAL GOODNESS

We have seen how moral discussion is relational as far as Scotus is concerned. It is founded on the natural law as its basis; it involves the two affections within the rational will; it involves the cooperation and collaboration of intellect and will. Moral goodness is also relational in an objective sense, that is, insofar as it depends upon an objective, natural goodness. This goodness is found in the natural order as created by God and as it perfects human rationality. For Scotus, if an act is not naturally good, it cannot be morally good. Telling the truth, for example, can only be morally good if there is some natural goodness about the truth. Truth is the object of the intellect and is the natural goal of reason. Because of this, telling the truth has potential for moral goodness precisely insofar as it has objective natural goodness.

Through his discussion of the foundation of the moral on the natural, along with his discussion of natural law as foundational to the moral order, Scotus grounds the objectivity of morals, first, on the divine will and, second, on human nature. In any moral choice or act, then, one should be able to identify the natural goodness of the bare act independently of anyone's choice of it or of any consideration of circumstances in which the act might be chosen or performed.

There are actions that can never be morally justified because they cannot be naturally justified: murder, adultery, deception, and perjury would be some examples. Every moral action must be justified on natural grounds before it can be justified on moral grounds. In Quodlibet 17,[31] Scotus traces the levels of goodness for a morally good act: the first level of goodness is natural/objective determined from the nature of the object and its relationship to the power. It answers the question: is this good in question a genuine good and object for rational choice? Once this question has been answered in the affirmative, one may pose a second question: is this good freely chosen by the will? This means: is this good moral in the sense of imputable to the agent? Is it an action for which the agent can be praised or blamed? Once this question is answered in the affirmative, one may proceed to the next question: is this action chosen and performed in accord with right reasoning and virtue? At this level, if all answers are affirmative, we are speaking of the fullest dimension of moral goodness: objective, voluntary, and rational.

In the example of telling the truth, for instance, we can proceed in the following manner: first, is truth an objective good for rationality and should it be chosen? Of course, the answer is yes. Second, in this particular situation do I choose to speak truthfully? Can this action be imputed to me as an agent in

control of my own actions? Third, having considered all aspects
of the present situation, is telling the truth in the particular
manner I do the result of a rational decision on my part to which
I agree? Have I met the various requirements–such as time,
place, manner–in this choice? Have I, for example, told the truth
in this particular situation at the right time, to the right person, and in the appropriate manner? Have I erred by telling too
much of the truth, or to the wrong person, or in a manner that is
not appropriate? The act has perfect goodness and, as such, is
fully imputable to me as a moral agent if I have fulfilled all the
conditions that such an act requires in such a situation. If, however, something is missing, then the act lacks some goodness or
a dimension of perfection it should have. Such an act is considered less than morally perfect, although it might still retain
some level of goodness. I can be praised for what I have done
but not praised for the way it was done. I can be blamed for not
observing an aspect of the situation I should have considered.
In such a case, although the act itself was good and even morally good, I should have known better than to do it in the way I
did.

My moral intention is among the most important dimensions
of the act, when it is fully considered as deserving of praise or
blame. Why I do what I do is just as important as what I do, and
more important than how I do it. If, for instance, I tell the truth
at the right time, with all the requirements of execution, and
yet do so to injure another, or to punish someone or take re-
venge, then my moral intention completely skews the entire act.
Now, it is in many ways a *different* act altogether. Such an act is
not lacking goodness in a deficient manner, but it is a perver-
sion of what should have been a good act. Such intentional vicious behavior is serious and twisted.

Scotus also entertains the possibility of what he calls an *undifferentiated* moral act.[32] This is an act whose moral dimension
is not fully specified because an important element, such as the
intention, is either missing or unclear. Here there is no perver-
sion of intent. There is no intent we can discern with sufficient
clarity to judge the sort of act this is. In such a case, the degree
of praise cannot be established.

We have then, four categories of moral determination. There is, first, the fully perfect moral action, where all appropriate aspects are present, the act itself is naturally good, freely chosen, with proper intention, rational and virtuous execution. There is, next, the imperfect moral act, where something is missing and the act is not as good as it could be. This act would possess badness *privatively*, as a deficiency of whatever goodness we might expect to find there. Third, there is the act that is perverted by an evil or vicious intention. This is the act that is willfully disordered. Finally, there is that undifferentiated or undetermined act whose intention is not conscious or clear enough to specify the act for its reward. While the third level would affect the person's character in a vicious way, the fourth would not affect it in any determined manner. In this sense, the undifferentiated act resembles an unreflected or unconscious act: it leaves no discernible moral imprint on the moral character of the person, because there is no moral intent to give it the sort of focus it would require for this.

CONCLUSIONS

This chapter has traced out the relationship that exists as the result of free choice, both in the divine and human wills. Such a relationship depends upon but is not reduced to the natural relatedness of order and the connection that manifests the beauty within creation, understood as a whole. The domain of divine free initiative, expressed in the history of salvation, the covenant, Incarnation, and Immaculate Conception offers itself to human reason for meditation and imitation.

This imitation defines the moral realm as the realm of human response to divine graciousness. It is a realm of rational freedom. More importantly, it is a realm of relationship and solidarity, freely undertaken, both by God and by us. It is in the affirmation of ordered loving that we most properly imitate the divine life of the Trinity and express that life to others. In the generosity of love, the human person expresses the deepest nature shared by means of the supreme act of divine initiative, the Incarnation. We are indeed *imago Dei* because we are *imago*

Christi, called to participate and to express the life of Trinitarian communion, freely and rationally. It is to this last, and most theological, dimension of Scotist thought that we now turn.

Notes

[1] As Scotus suggests in his discussion of *potentia absoluta* and *potentia ordinata* in *Ordinatio* I, 44 (VI:363-369) translated in *Duns Scotus on the Will and Morality* (1986), 254-260.

[2] Scotus explains divine intention in this way: "Hence, he first loves himself ordinately and consequently not inordinately in an envious or jealous manner. Secondly, he wills to have co-lovers, and this is nothing else than willing that others have his love in themselves....Thirdly, however, he wills those things which are necessary to attain his end, namely, the gift of grace." Cited by Wolter in *Duns Scotus on the Will and Morality*, 20, taken from *Reportatio* IA, d. 44, q. 2.

[3] *De Primo Principio* 1.2 (2).

[4] This term was coined by E. Gilson and is used to refer to the medieval reflection upon being and the way that reflection offered a way to speak of God with human language. The term reveals the particular way medieval philosophy and theology had converging intuitions around Aristotelian philosophy.

[5] *Francis of Assisi: Early Documents*, vol I: The Saint (Hyde Park, NY: New City Press, 1999), 131.

[6] This insight regarding *christification* also appears in Bonaventure, both in his approach in the *Legenda Major* and in his *Sermones de diversis,* J-G. Bougerol, ed., (Paris: Editions Franciscaines,1993), Sermo IV, 783. See Jacques Delarun's discussion of this in *The Misadventure of Francis of Assisi,* Edw. Hagman, trans., (St. Bonaventure NY: Franciscan Institute Publications, 2002), 230-231.

[7] *Ordinatio* III, d. 7, 3. This text is reproduced and translated in Allan Wolter's *Four Questions on Mary*, The Franciscan Institute, 2000, 20-27. See Appendix 2, 172-91.

[8] *Ordinatio I,* d. 41, unica (VI: 312-339). Scotus refers to this text in the body of his argument in III, d. 7, 3.

[9] *Ordinatio* III, d. 7, 3 in *Four Questions on Mary*, 25.

[10] *Francis of Assisi: Early Documents*, vol I: 132-133.

[11] See St. Francis de Sales, *The Treatise on the Love of God,* II, ch. 2-4 (Westminister, MD: The Newman Book Shop, 1942), 66-76. Bernadette Waterman Ward offers an excellent study of the importance of Scotist thought in the life and poetry of Hopkins in *World As Word: Philosophical Theology in Gerard Manley Hopkins* (Washington, D.C.: Catholic University of America Press, 2001), 131-197.

[12]*Francis of Assisi: Early Documents*, vol I: 131-132.

[13]His explanation of the two orders, intention and execution, relies upon the analogy with the artist in the act of creative execution. See *Ordinatio* III, d. 7, 3 in *Four Questions on Mary*, 25.

[14]The feast of the Immaculate Conception, December 8, is placed exactly nine months before the Feast of the Birth of Mary, September 8. In like manner, the Annunciation, March 25, is nine months before Christmas.

[15]*Ordinatio* III, d. 3, 1, reproduced and translated by Allan Wolter in *Four Questions on Mary*, 35-62. See Appendix 2, 172-91.

[16]This was a traditional Franciscan position, beginning with Alexander of Hales, John Rupella, et al. In their interpretation of original sin, the early Franciscan intellectual tradition preferred Anselm's discussion of the loss of original justice in the soul to Augustine's infected flesh model. For an excellent presentation of these early positions, see Wolter's "The Doctrine of the Immaculate Conception in the Early Franciscan School" *Proceedings of the Marian Congress*, 1954, 26-69.

[17]I consider the moral dimension of Scotist thought according to the relationship of mutuality in *The Harmony of Goodness: Mutuality and Moral Living According to John Duns Scotus*, (Quincy IL: Franciscan Press, 1996). In that study, I consider all the moral elements in much greater detail.

[18]This text is reproduced and translated in Allan Wolter, *Duns Scotus on the Will and Morality*, 268-287. See Appendix 2, 172-91.

[19]See John 14:22.

[20]On this, see Richard Cross, *Duns Scotus*, Great Medieval Thinkers Series (New York: Oxford University Press, 1999), 89-91.

[21]I develop this insight in light of Scotus's renewed anthropology in "Duns Scotus, Morality and Happiness–A Reply to Thomas Williams" in *American Catholic Philosophical Quarterly*, 2000 (74): 173-195.

[22]This discussion appears in *Ordinatio* II, d. 6, 2 translated in *Duns Scotus on the Will and Morality*, 462-477. Allan Wolter's seminal

discussion of freedom in Scotus appears in "Native Freedom of the Will: A Key to the Ethics of Scotus," *The Philosophical Theology of John Duns Scotus*, Marilyn M. Adams, ed.. (Cornell, NY: Cornell University Press, 1990), 148-162. See Appendix 2, 172-91.

[23]See my "Duns Scotus, Morality and Happiness...," 183-187.

[24]His *Questions on the Metaphysics of Aristotle*, IX, q. 15 of which the relevant translated passage can be found in *Duns Scotus on the Will and Morality*, 144-173. See Appendix 2, 172 91.

[25]Immanuel Kant's *Foundations for a Metaphysics of Morals* begins with this distinction.

[26]In his work on Scotus, Thomas Williams appears to overlook the crucial importance of self-consciousness and moral self-awareness present in Scotus's arguments. Williams goes no further than the notion of freedom as undetermined behavior and concludes that even God's exercise of freedom is radically independent of any discernible content. This is made worse by his choice to disregard Scotus's more theological discussions of freedom in God and, additionally, the fact that Scotus lived and worked within a religious tradition. Thus, in his "How Scotus Separates Morality from Happiness" (*ACPQ* 1995 (69): 425-445) and "The Unmitigated Scotus" (*Archiv für Geschichte der Philosophie* 1998 (80): 162-181), I believe he interprets Scotist thought independently of any relevant spiritual context.

[27]This text has its own history where the critical discussion is concerned. Scotus left this question (and those surrounding it) out of the *Ordinatio*, clearly intending to return to them at a later time. Because of his early death, he never had a chance to lay this position out in final form. At the present, scholars work with the *Lectura* and *Reportatio* versions of this text. Here, as noted in the first chapter, is a key point of debate and discussion among the contemporary scholarly community. Detailed discussion of this would be far beyond the scope of the present work. Of interest would be Stephen Dumont's "Did Scotus Change His Mind on the Will?" in *After the Condemnation of 1277: Philosophy and Theology at the University of Paris in the Last Quarter of the Thirteenth Century,* Jan Aertsen, Kent Emery, Jr., and Andreas Speer, eds. (Berlin: Walter de Gruyter, 2001), 719-94 and my "Did Scotus Modify His Position on the Relation of Intellect and Will?" in *Recherches de Théologie et Philosophie Médiévales,* 69, 1 (2002): 88-116.

[28]I discuss this more carefully in "Practical Wisdom: Scotus's Presentation of Prudence" in *John Duns Scotus: Metaphysics and Ethics*, Ludger Honnefelder, Rega Wood, Mechtild Dreyer, eds., (Leiden: Brill, 1996), 551-571.

[29]Scotus refers to Augustine's comment, "Nothing is more in the power of the will than the will itself" (*Retractions* I, c. 9 (8), PL 32, 596) in *Quodlibet* 18, n. 11, 18.28 in *God and Creatures*, 408.

[30]This is also part of Williams' interpretation of Scotus. See note 26 above.

[31]A translation of this text appears in *God and Creatures: The Quodlibetal Questions*, Alluntis/Wolter, eds. (Princeton, NJ: Princeton University Press, 1975), 388-398.

[32]Sometimes called the morally indifferent act. See *Ordinatio* II, d.41, reproduced in *Duns Scotus on the Will and Morality*, 228-234.

Chapter 4

Communion

The Franciscan emphasis on love is the final aspect for our study of the thought of John Duns Scotus. This is not to say that only in the Franciscan tradition do we find love as the fullest culmination of human life. Indeed, this affirmation of the primacy of charity is proper to Christianity and is acknowledged by all Christian thinkers, even the most "intellectualist" among them. For this present volume, the way the primacy of love or charity underpins the entire Franciscan vision has significance. Indeed, the perspective of charity re-frames every discussion around the affective rationality of the human person as one who mirrors the divine reality of Triune Communion.[1]

The Franciscan spiritual tradition encompasses not only the writings of Francis but also the early documents from Clare of Assisi. In a blessing attributed to Clare, we read: "Always be lovers of God and your souls and the souls of your sisters, and always be eager to observe what you have promised the Lord."[2] As this passage affirms, the sort of love that inspires this spiritual tradition involves a three-fold dimension: love for God, love for one another in community and, finally, fidelity to a commitment made. We find all three aspects in Scotus's discussion of Trinitarian life. They flow forth from God's dynamic inner life to the life of all. Not only is love for God the ground of all reality, but that same love can inform our love for others. Such a love imitates divine artistry: it is generous, creative of relationship and, most importantly, faithful despite inevitable infidelity, betrayal and rejection.

Before we begin a consideration of the how the life of the Trinity grounds all reality, let us take a moment to reflect upon the difference between a framework based on knowledge and one based on love. Each framework has its own understanding of the triadic relationship between the person, the activity and the object. For the framework based on knowledge, we find the knower (the person), the known (the object) and the act of understanding (the activity). For the framework based upon love, we have the lover, the beloved and the act of love. Since we want to see both perspectives in the best light possible, let us call the act of understanding the highest act of cognition, where the knower sees, to the highest degree possible, the reality of the object as it truly is. And, let us call the act of love the act of the *affectio iustitiae*, that is, the highest affection of the rational will, that by which I love the beloved on the basis of his or her intrinsic value and not on the basis of whatever good the beloved might bring me. Wisdom (knowledge) and Charity (love), then, are the two perspectives at play here. Both express something of the reality of the rational order. Both are relational and both are significant. They are not mutually exclusive, but offer two distinct ways of viewing reality and its relationship to human, rational response. Given this, why might a thinker like Scotus choose charity over wisdom to ground his perspective?

A clear preference for the one over the other comes from a reflection upon the perfective activity and its distinguishing characteristics. In this way, if the goal of the life of knowledge, of intellectual contemplation is to understand, then the goal of affective longing is communion. While both the act of understanding and the act of loving result in union with the object, the nature of this union is expressed differently. When the act of understanding *unites* the knower with the known the union lies within the knower. The activity is framed by the nature of the knower. When I understand something, I consider it within my own consciousness, I refer it to other things I already know, I make it mine. This does not necessarily mean that I reduce it completely to my own subjectivity, nor that understanding is disconnected from the world outside my mind. It simply means that the act of understanding always depends more upon the possibilities and capacities within the mind of the person who understands than it does on the reality of what is understood. For instance, a child does not understand mathematics in the way an adult might. Neither would understand math as a university professor would. And yet, in the case of the child, the adult and the professional mathematician, the domain of mathematics does not change. What makes each act of understanding different is determined by the one who is thinking (child, adult, professional) and not by the fact that the numbers are different for someone who is less able to understand their relationship.

For the limited, finite human mind, attempting to understand all reality is like trying to put the ocean into an eight-ounce glass. When the glass is full, the glass is full, even though a lot of water remains outside the glass. The insight Augustine is said to have had when he contemplated how the human mind might understand the Trinity takes on full force here. When it comes to the divine reality, and perhaps to all reality, one can never know the fullness of what is there to be known.

In the act of loving, by contrast, the union achieved is fundamentally *ecstatic*, or outside the lover. When I love another in the best manner possible, according to the highest love, I do not make the other *mine* in any sense. This is precisely the difference between the *affectio iustitiae* and the *affectio commodi*. Rather, I am united with the other in an act that is both mine and takes me beyond myself. Perfect love is not possessive, but self-transcending and creative of relationship. The highest act of love embraces both an immanent and a transcendent dimension. It takes the lover out of himself in union with the beloved. It is an act whose dynamism never ends. In the case of reciprocal love, the relational dynamic continues to feed the union. And the union never ceases to deepen.

There are several additional reasons why Scotus prefers the framework of love over that of knowledge as definitive, both of reality as a whole, but also of the perfection of human rational-

ity. First, and most obviously, the Franciscan tradition is profoundly indebted to Augustine. Augustine himself embraced a
vision founded on ordered loving as well as a moral perspective
that is both deeply Platonic and aesthetic in nature. Second,
the tradition as a whole emphasized the affective dimension of
human rationality over the intellectual dimension. Alexander
of Hales, Bonaventure, William of Ware, and Peter John Olivi
all began with the primacy of love over knowledge, especially
given the consequences of original sin and the broken, clouded
stated of human cognition that resulted. Bonaventure's thought
is deeply imbued with a Platonic and aesthetic cast, acknowl-
edging the divine reality as Beauty beyond description. Finally,
the insight of Francis and Clare of Assisi into the beauty of the
created world and into the human response in love makes such
a preference natural. To such a great gift, one could respond
with an act of understanding and assent, but an act of gratitude
and love would be vastly superior.

When Scotus focuses on the will and its exercise of freedom,
we should more properly understand this in terms of the
Franciscan focus on the power of love, in whose perfection lies
the fullness of the human person as rational image of God. Too
often such a focus on the will can suggest either a focus on arbitrary *willfulness*, or a type of irrational unpredictability that
can be read into various Scotist texts where he defends the power
and superiority of the will over the intellect. This is because
today we tend to separate our understanding of freedom from a
notion of rationality. When Scotus claims that the will is superior to the intellect, it is far too tempting to understand this as
a claim about the superiority of freedom over rationality. As we
have seen earlier in his re-casting of rationality within the will,
this is *precisely* not what Scotus claims. It is therefore helpful
(and sobering) for us to remember that medieval thinkers do
not always understand terms in the way that we do.

If, however, we take seriously the Franciscan dimension to
Scotus's texts and read beyond a literal interpretation to see
the heart of his approach, we note that here is a different vision
of what it means to be human and to be rational. If, as this
tradition suggests, the fullest perfection of the human person

involves love, and right or ordered loving, then *rationality* must be seen to involve more than *problem-solving* and *analysis*. It involves the recognition of intrinsic worth (as Chapter 2 showed), the nature of relationships (as Chapter 3 made clear), and the aesthetic dimension at the heart of reality. It highlights synthesis rather than analysis, integration rather than fragmentation.

This tradition also emphasizes a particular vision of the divinity in whose image the human person is created. Accordingly, God would be understood less as omnipotent, omniscient and transcendent and more as generosity, mercy and conserving presence. To love in an ordered manner (as God loves) is to give oneself without end, to be endlessly creative of reality and relationship. God's nature is that of the Artist who never tires of inventing creative and generous responses to human actions. The goal of such a perspective would be union with God, understood not as the *beatific vision,* but rather as the *beatific embrace*.[3]

GOD'S ESSENCE AS TRIUNE UNITY

Scotus's vision of reality is profoundly Trinitarian and relational. Indeed, the Trinity exemplifies both the dynamism of love that Scotus identifies at the heart of rationality and the free outpouring of generosity that enables him to affirm that, in God, justice and mercy coincide. When we reflect upon the nature of God as Triune Unity, we plumb the depths of what it might mean to say we are created in the image of God, as icons of the divine, as *imago Dei*.

God's inner nature holds the key to the relationship of love and mutuality to which all are called. This inner dynamic of divine life and love, God's activity *ad intra*, constitutes the divine nature: it is the necessity proper to God. God's loving self-relationship is both necessary (because God is the highest good and worthy of infinite love) and free (since love belongs to the will – a free potency – and, additionally, since God delights in loving).[4] Without this dynamic God would not be God. When Scotus reflects upon the relational dimension of the divine nature in *Quodlibetal Question* 4,[5] he explains how the essence of

God (one *per se* being) involves both an incommunicable dimension proper to each person (three "incommunicable subsistents"),[6] along with a communal dimension that can only be described within a relationship and by means of the technical language of relationship.[7]

As a logician, Scotus approaches this incommunicable dimension of each divine person as the *suppositum*, or logical term, necessary for any discussion of relationship. In other words, in the sentence: "John is the brother of Paul," the term *John* is both the subject of the sentence and the *suppositum* or logical term that grounds the relationship to Paul (a second *suppositum*); their relationship is expressed by the term *brother.* One could not imagine the familial relationship of brotherhood for a child who had no siblings. There is no one to whom to be a brother. Or, at least, if there were a *suppositum*, it would be the non-existent brother, or the imaginary brother, or the brother the child wished she had had, but did not. Language, then, and especially the language of all relationship expressed in logical predication, requires some type of fixed term that functions as subject or object, of which the relationship can be predicated.

When we apply this to God, we see that, from a purely logical point of view, the three persons of the Trinity–Father, Son and Spirit–must function as the *supposita*, or basic terms, that ground the relational language of *paternity, generation and spiration*. These terms must have the sort of *logical* independence required for predication of properties that express relationship. The Father is not the Son. The relationship of fatherhood or sonship requires such a distinction. If there were no distinction between the two, then there would be no relationship: there would be identity. Because relational properties such as these can only be understood of one thing in terms of another, one needs a foundational logical term that grounds the relationship. Without such a fixed term, the mind would have nothing on which to ground the relationship; language could not express anything about the divine nature.

In terms of each person of the Trinity, such distinctive existence cannot be captured by the term *haecceitas*, used earlier to denote individuating principle. The Persons of the Trinity do not each enjoy a different *haec*. *Haecceitas*, it will be remembered, is the ultimate specific difference, beyond which there is no individuation. It individuates and separates. Such individuals always exist independently of one another. This is not true of the persons of the Trinity. Scotus never uses this term to refer to God or to the persons in the Trinity. In speaking of the Trinity, he relies on the Victorine tradition to point to the incommunicable dimension of each of the three.[8] This refers to what the First Person cannot communicate to the Second, nor to the Third. This dimension is expressed in relational language as *paternity*.

Because of his primarily logical consideration of this question, Scotus actually offered an early consideration of the Trinity that was not entirely in harmony with the common opinion. According to the traditional standard Augustinian interpretation (found in the *De Trinitate*), the personhood of each divine person is constituted by the relationship to the other two. For Augustine, God's essence is relationship. For Scotus, God's essence is persons in relationship. In his earliest *(Lectura)* discussion of the relationship of the persons in the Trinity (in I, distinction 26), Scotus defended the absolute constitution of the first person, in the absence of any discussion of relationship. Each divine person, he argued, is indeed a person in an absolute sense *(per modos essendi)* and not relative to the other two *(per relationes)*. When it comes to human speculation upon God, however, there are only two truths that must be held: first, that there are three persons in one God, and second, that the first produces the second and the first two produce the third. Beyond these two aspects of the divine nature, any other question (for example, whether the personhood of each is relative or absolute, as he argued) remains open.[9]

In his later *Ordinatio* version of this text,[10] while Scotus acknowledged the possibility of the traditional teaching, he emphasized that the divine persons, even when we can conceive of them *per modos essendi*, cannot be understood in absence from their mutual relationships. These relationships must be essential (and not accidental) to the divine persons, in order to safeguard divine simplicity. Indeed, the essence of God is always to

be explained in terms that the human intellect can grasp, however vaguely, the truth about God. When Jesus spoke of his Father, then, he used the language of relationship to express his
union with the First Person. He could not have done otherwise,
since anything one can say about God that is descriptive in nature requires some sort of relational language.

Scotus's insights about the Trinity as relational communion
ground his entire vision of reality. Like God, all that is exists in
relationship and is ordered toward everything else. Like God,
each being possesses an incommunicable individuality (which
for us would refer to our *haecceitas*) that lies beyond language
but still serves as the basis for language and description. At the
highest point of all that exists, there is a being whose oneness is
communion. This communion is simple, generative and life- giving. Communion and mutual self-gift define the perfection of
divine being. It is therefore relationship rather than autonomy
that best fulfills the human desire for happiness and best perfects human rationality. In its fullness, our human experience
of relationship and mutuality images the life of God.

GOD'S ACTION AD EXTRA: THE ORDER OF MERIT

At the highest level of Scotus's discussion of human action we
find the order of merit. This dimension of reality is framed by
the relationship of communion between God and the individual
human person. *Merit* is constituted by charity (love) and is dou-
bly defined. From the human side merit refers to the act insofar
as it is informed by the intention of love for God. Because of this
loving intention, the act is itself *finalized* toward the highest
and most perfect good. From the divine side, the meritorious act
is also framed in love. Here, divine loving acceptance rewards
the human act with a divine response.

Merit is a reciprocal relationship of loving friendship between
the person and God. The meritorious act lies between two free
and loving wills. It is (as it were) suspended between the loving
freedom that performs it and the loving freedom that rewards
it. As a focus for two loving regards, the meritorious act is constituted by the reciprocal relationship of love. Indeed, where

merit is concerned, charity is the foundation, the intention, the result, and the reward. A reflection on the order of merit reveals the centrality of love and generosity in Scotus's vision of the relationship between the human and divine wills.[11]

In order to proceed in this, it is perhaps best to move more carefully one step at a time. We begin with a consideration of divine action and then move to a discussion of human action. First, let us consider the Trinity and the divine relationship to all that is not God. As we have seen, divine activity internal to the Trinity (*ad intra*) is necessary. It is also free. In God, necessity and freedom are not mutually exclusive. Since God is the highest good, and since good must be loved, then God's self-love is a necessary characteristic of divine inner life. However, the action of God relative to all else that exists (or *ad extra*) is free (contingent), but not necessary. Since beyond God, there is no being equal to God, then there is no being that necessarily requires divine love. When God loves or creates *ad extra* such an act is free of any constraint or necessity. In addition, all God does *ad extra* is informed solely by divine integrity and intention. Since all perfections are one in God and since the divine nature is utterly simple, divine activity knows no reason external to itself. This foundational affirmation of divine autonomy appeared earlier in our discussion both of creation and, in particular, of the Incarnation. The Word did not become flesh because of the sin of Adam, or for any reason that necessitated God's action in a way to force or constrain divine behavior.

Something still seems amiss here. This aspect of divine life gives rise to two sets of questions. The first set deals with the relationship of freedom to necessity. How can freedom and necessity co-exist in any being? One is free precisely when one does not have to act of necessity. Indeed, Scotus himself used the distinction between necessary and free causal activity to explain and defend moral behavior. It seems odd now to affirm that, in God, both freedom and necessity coexist. A second set of questions deals with the distinction between the inner life of God and what goes on outside of God, as well as the divine relationship to all reality. How might we best understand the coincidence of freedom and necessity in God but not outside God?

Why does the same necessity of divine self-relationship not apply to beings outside of God, beings that God has created and created out of love?

Let us begin with the first set of questions: namely, how can freedom and necessity coexist in a being? How might an act be understood to be both free and necessary? Scotus affirms simply that, in God, freedom and necessity are both operative, because of the nature of God and the nature of love. Indeed, such coexistence is not logically impossible. One can find examples of events in which free choice and necessity do indeed coincide. Scotus takes an example from Cicero, offering the case of suicide, where one might throw oneself over a precipice. Here the actual fall of the person would be necessary and according to the requirements of nature. The attraction of the weight of the body to the center of the earth and the force of gravity both operate according to natural necessity. A falling body could not stop without being impeded. If there were a rock formation midway down the precipice, for example, the person's fall would be broken. The fall is a necessary event. However, if the person, in falling, also intended to fall and to fall to his death, then the act of falling would also be a voluntary act and therefore free.[12]

As this example applies to God, an analogous situation occurs. As the highest good, God cannot not be loved, not even by God. Here is the natural dimension of divine self-relationship. But God's nature is love. This means that God cannot not act out of the divine will. In acting out of the divine will, God's actions are intended and chosen, undetermined by anything external to the divine. God's acts are therefore free and the act of divine self-love is also free. In acting graciously, that is, according to the divine nature, God freely intends to act and freely chooses to act in accordance with the divine perfections. Hence, the divine activity reveals both necessity and freedom in the divine essence.

Answering this first set of questions actually helps us answer the second set. Since freedom (as we have seen) is independent from external constraint, one is free to act when one is not constrained or forced by anyone or anything external to oneself. Clearly, the inner life of the Trinity is free in precisely this sense.

God's inner life of love is defined on the basis of the autonomous divine nature: completely self-contained in its intentional objects. But divine activity exhibits just this sort of intentional independence when acting *ad extra*. What is not identical is the nature of the object. No created object possesses the good belonging to the divine nature. Therefore, God's freedom *ad extra* is, in itself, no different from that same freedom *ad intra*. The difference comes from the object. External to the divine essence there is no natural reason belonging to any course of action that would constrain or necessitate divine choice. Any actions God takes outside the divine essence are not completely explainable in terms of conditions, objects or situations that exist independently of God.

However, just because there is no external way to justify or explain divine action, this does not mean that the actions cannot be explained. These actions can be explained, however, precisely in terms of divine identity, divine integrity, and divine intentionality. These three point to the metaphysical necessity that requires that, whatever the being in question, that being must always be that being, and not another. Simply put: whatever God chooses to do, God cannot not be God, nor would God act in a way counter to divine nature.

Concretely, this means that, in any situation involving divine action, one cannot completely explain the situation solely in terms of the conditions within which God has acted. We must allow for a partial explanation coming from the nature of God. Why God chose Abram, for example, cannot be completely explained in terms of Abram's character or natural traits. Why God remained faithful to the Hebrews and Israelites despite their infidelity is a question that can only be completely answered by an appeal to the divine nature and to the requirements of gracious love that flows from God's self-identity and integrity. Such an explanation need not be based on an appeal to divine unpredictability or arbitrary spontaneity. Rather, the explanation takes full advantage of the divine nature as love, and of the metaphysical requirements that flow, naturally and freely, from such a being.

All this points to a central dimension to divine love and freedom: *firmitas* or divine steadfastness.[13] As we saw earlier in the distinction between *potentia absoluta dei* and *potentia ordinata dei*, God's choice to act within a certain established order is itself an affirmation of the divine commitment to the prior choice to establish that order. The divine choice expresses the "ability to adhere to its object in a self-actualizing action, the love-product of which is in no way pre-figured in the will nor coerced by the object."[14] This sort of divine fidelity is both the deepest expression of divine nature and the fullest manifestation of the exercise of creative freedom.

Because divine identity and integrity are so important in our understanding the true nature of divine freedom, Scripture is the essential backdrop for Scotist thought. Freedom and necessity come together in God, once we realize the sort of God Scotus is reflecting upon as he discusses the perfection of freedom in the divine will. Understood as divine self-revelation themselves, the sacred Scriptural texts give us critical information about the nature of God. This information both lies behind and helps explain divine action in human history. Salvation history recounts in a marvelous manner the details of divine activity *ad extra*: the call of Abram, the Exodus, the Incarnation. These actions both recount and predict divine response. What God has revealed in the past can be used as a basis for the human expectation for the future. For Scotus, it is not the *fact* of divine graciousness and fidelity that is at issue; it is the *extent* of divine graciousness and fidelity that cannot be assigned ahead of time.

The movement of divine graciousness of which the Incarnation is the fullest manifestation culminates in the divine response of *acceptatio* in the order of merit. Here is the act of love by which God *accepts* any human action as worthy of reward and orders it toward whatever manner of fulfillment that is deemed suitable according to divine generosity. In the *Ordinatio* Prologue, for example, Scotus refers to the example of the honorable pagan, someone who does what is right on the basis of his conscience alone, and not on the basis of any knowledge of scripture or what God wants. Such a person, Scotus points out, could be accepted *de congruo*, on the basis of divine *potentia absoluta,* since the action would be in harmony with what a believer would do in the same instance. The reward for this person would be a deepened relationship to God, even if he were not completely aware of the nature of the divine being as revealed in Scripture.[15]

Earlier in this important opening question to the *Ordinatio* Prologue,[16] Scotus had contrasted his position with that of the philosophers involved in the controversy over the necessity of revelation. These philosophers (who were apparently meant to stand in for those teaching at the Faculty of Arts at the close of the thirteenth century) held to a vision of human fulfillment completely based on the Aristotelian model of intellectual speculation and the understanding of God as Thought Thinking Itself. In his response Scotus argues that the divine essence (*deitas*) is proper to theological discourse because theology has access to sacred texts. Such texts make a claim to the authority of divine inspiration. They offer information about the divine internal life that philosophers such as Aristotle cannot fathom. It is quite different to pray to a God who is Thought Itself, rather than Triune communion of gracious generosity. Once we come to know the true nature of God, then all aspects of human reflection are transformed in the divine image. Philosophers and theologians depicted in the *Prologue* understand God differently. This difference of perspective makes all the difference. When Scotus affirms that whatever God might do in any given situation, God must be God, he is making a theological claim about divine nature and action. He is making a claim the fullest meaning of which derives from reflection upon Scripture. He is *not* appealing to the unknowability of divine action in the face of which the person is helpless.

A lived relationship with God in prayer results in a particular insight into the divine motivation, based upon one's own lived experience. We can easily find a parallel for this sort of insight in our own lives. Suppose my very good friend, whose faithfulness has been tested, offers to surprise me for my birthday. Now, I can count on this friend and have counted on this friend in the past. Here is someone who has helped me in difficult times and, as much as possible, has been present in my life as a support and confidant. How could I be afraid? Why would I be afraid? What do I know about this friend that would give me any reason to be apprehensive about the upcoming day? Rather, I would look forward to it with anxious anticipation, knowing that, whatever this friend comes up with, it's going to be good.

When Scotus discusses the order of merit, he situates it in the theological domain, because it depends upon the nature of God, precisely as revealed in Scripture. When he speaks of *acceptatio*, Scotus assumes that the God referred to is one that we know well both from our reflection upon scripture and upon our own personal experiences. This is a God who can be trusted. *Acceptatio* appears as the culmination of divine intentionality from the first moment. There is no distinction between the graciousness of the creator, the redeemer, and sanctifier. Nothing, not even human weakness, has interfered with the realization of divine desire. Indeed, history unfolds as single movement of love that informs human experience. *Acceptatio* is nothing less than the bringing to completion of the good work begun by God at the moment when order came forth out of chaos. As ordered and ordering love, it is part of the overall divine intention to reveal and share graciousness and mercy. Like divine action recorded in Scripture, the act of acceptance expresses the divine joy and, in particular, the delight with which God responds to every human action. *Acceptatio* is the divine applause for human efforts at loving; the divine joy at the sight of human generosity. In *acceptatio*, God's freedom meets human freedom; God's love encounters human love. In *acceptatio*, God freely and lovingly embraces a human action performed out of love. This action, however great or small, is accepted and rewarded. Indeed, where the order of merit is concerned, Scotus affirms only one certainty: God's freedom and love are so immense that we can count on a reward far beyond anything our actions deserve. Divine goodness does not stop there, since our punishment for our sins will also be far less than we deserve.[17]

Now let us address this question of merit from the perspective of the human. Scotus presents the order of merit as lying between the highest order of moral perfection and the order of the divine.[18] It is defined by love, since the difference between an act that is morally perfect (that is, completely in accord with right reason and performed in a morally appropriate manner) and an act that is meritorious is the fact that the meritorious act is informed (or inspired) by love for God. This act, done out of charity, always receives the highest reward: the divine response of delight. In the order of merit, the vertical ascent of human desire and action encounters the divine descent of love and generosity. The two free potencies converge on the charitable act. The divine and human wills unite in this object of love. The human will places the object before the Lord who lovingly accepts it. In this loving acceptance, both the object and the human person are caught up into divine life.

According to Scotus, the highest human perfection is not justice, or even acting out of the affection for justice. This is the fulfillment of moral perfection, but not yet a perfection that shares in divine life. Rather, the highest perfection is love, and generous love in imitation of God's outpouring in creation, redemption, and salvation. So, for example, while I would certainly be pleased if my friend (described above) threw me a surprise party because I had thrown one for her (and justice would require such reciprocity), I'd much rather have her throw me a party out of friendship and love, and not out of justice. The two intentions (justice and charity) do in fact make the actions different. An act performed out of love is superior to one performed out of justice because it imitates the divine action and is never limited by the constraints of what is required. Indeed, divine action goes beyond justice to us because generosity is never limited merely to what we deserve.

Divine *acceptatio* is the manifestation of generous freedom according to a Franciscan perspective. Just as Francis was free to throw all his possessions away and rely completely on the love of God, so God is free to throw caution to the wind, as it were, and toss out rewards, not so much to the completely undeserving (since God can never reward the sinner for sin, nor punish the good person for being good),[19] but far beyond the actual amount that might be determined in a calculation of strict justice. This sort of God is depicted in the parable told by Jesus in Matthew 20: the generous master who pays everyone the same amount at the end of the day, and wonders why some complain because he is generous.

When, therefore, Scotus exalts the action of the divine will in his texts, it is not the defense of an arbitrary God upon whom we cannot count or depend. Rather, it is the affirmation of the divinity of generosity, a defense of the Franciscan penchant to throw caution to the wind. This is what it means to rely *"mere ex voluntate Dei"* – solely on the divine will – which really means solely on divine love and generosity.

Generosity is thus rendered rational; indeed, it is rationality itself. In the generous act, the person pours forth, not unreflectively nor because of any external constraint or condition that requires action of a particular sort, but because this is what it means to be that sort of person. Here generosity meets integrity, as the deepest reality of the divinity is generous and intentional love, mercy, and forgiveness. The reason God acts in this way, Scotus would argue, is because this is the sort of person (or Triune communion) that God is. This God is clearly *not* the God of the Philosophers, or the intellectuals of his time. It is not the God of Aristotle or Plato: a God understood to be Ground of Being, Unmoved Mover, Necessary Principle or Form of the Good. These gods are fine for others, but they do not hold a candle to the triune God revealed in Jesus Christ. And here, Scotus argues, Christianity has something that really is Good News.

Indeed, this God is not best encountered by thinking or speculating about the divine nature: not a God of theory at all.[20] This is a personal God encountered by and in the activity of loving and selfless generosity: a God of *praxis*, a dynamic God to be encountered not possessed; a God into whose inner life we are invited and whose sole desire is to transform us into our true selves, as genuine and vibrant *imago Dei*. This God is frightening. Here is not someone to carry around in a purse or wallet. This is a demanding, irritating, relentless "Hound of Heaven" sort of God, who never leaves us where we'd rather stay and always calls us further and deeper into the reality of love, generosity, and mercy.

In a beautiful argument in IV, 46, Scotus considers how it is that God's justice is mercy.[21] In answer to the question of the

coincidence of justice and mercy, especially in forgiveness of sinners, Scotus begins with a presentation of two notions of justice.
The first is from Anselm, the second from Aristotle. The first
(Anselmian) understanding of justice involves rectitude of the
will served for its own sake. The second (Aristotelian) understanding of the term deals with this rectitude in relationship to
another. In other words, there is a sense of justice that refers to
the self, to what character and integrity require. Additionally,
there is a sense of justice that involves due proportion to something or someone other than oneself, giving someone what he
deserves. An act may be just in either or both senses. I can act
justly toward myself as well as toward another.[22]

So, in the case of divine justice, we can consider the following
situation: God could act by virtue of either perspective. God can
either respond according to the object (what it deserves) or according to the divine nature (what God owes the divine nature,
so to speak). Clearly, God's integrity far exceeds any demands
the external object might make on divine action. God's deepest
justice then, is justice to divine integrity.[23] God must always be
God, regardless of the circumstance. This is the metaphysical
requirement of divine identity. When, however, we remember
that the creature is what it is because of the prior act of divine
choice, God's action according to the divine nature is in harmony with the earlier divine creative action that brought this
creature into being. So, even when God does act out of Anselm's
sense of justice, the creature is still getting what it deserves
*because the deepest value of that being has already been given
by God.* To say that such a being receives what it deserves is not
to say it merits on its own. Indeed, what it deserves belongs to
the order of created goodness chosen by God in love.[24] What had
appeared as two different perspectives on justice now collapses
into one, in light of the divine nature and the original act of
divine desire to create this world. There is still more good news:
since God's nature is love and generosity, this means quite simply that God's justice is mercy, forgiveness, and generosity. For
this reason, we cannot know what reward awaits us, for indeed,
"eye has not seen, nor has ear heard, what God has stored up
for those who love him" (1 Cor. 2:9).

Finally, divine *acceptatio* reveals the aesthetic dimension of Scotist thought. In his presentation of the divine response in the order of merit, Scotus likens it to the pleasure experienced by one who listens to beautiful music.[25] In *Lectura* and *Ordinatio* I, dist. 17, Scotus explains that just as harmony is pleasing to the listener, the fullest human action (where moral goodness is informed by love) possesses the fullest harmony and is, therefore, most pleasing to the divine ear. In both texts, Scotus develops the relationship of the morally good act as harmoniously ordered whole.[26] Just as the chords of a harp are the result of the harmonious blending of the various strings, played in a particular order that is itself beautiful, so the overall chord is constituted by an objective relationship of ordering of its parts.[27] This objective relationship of goodness has its subjective counterpart in the receptive divine ear.

"GOD IS TO BE LOVED" AS FOUNDATIONAL PRINCIPLE

The foundational principle for all reality, "God is to be loved" now reveals itself more fully as a relational and reciprocal principle. At this level, God is loved not so much as the highest good, but as the most gracious being who rewards us far beyond anything we might do to deserve it. If God has initiated and established such a relationship with us, then the only human response possible is gratitude. By this act of gratitude, the person strengthens the relationship initiated by God but now reaffirmed by human love in return. The circle is complete: from God to us, from us to God, then back to us and back to God. The order of all reality in relationship to God is dynamic movement, not static. There is, consequently, only one first principle for all action, whether human or divine. That principle is both first and final principle, Alpha and Omega. The principle functions as both the beginning of relationship and its culmination in communion of God with all persons, among all persons and then back to God. As it applies to God, this principle defines the life of the Trinity as interpersonal communion. All that God does is inspired by the divine love that is the free and intentional outpouring of the life of the Trinity.[28] As it applies to all reality, this principle expresses the communion of all with and in God.

Since, as we saw earlier, human rationality is framed in love, then this principle is foundational to the person as rational and is, as it were, "written on the human heart" in the manner that all first principles are intrinsic to rationality. The human *heart* has Biblical echoes,[29] referring to the deepest point of the human person. It does not refer primarily to human emotions. Thus, the natural and rational human desire to recognize, be drawn toward and love what is good is deeply engrained in human nature. It is the human *capax Dei*, our restless heart of which Augustine speaks so eloquently.[30]

This sort of love at the highest divine level does not make God selfish or narcissistic, but rather joyous and happy. God's love is not inwardly focused because, even if it were, God is a community of persons. For God, the inward focus is an outward focus, an inclusive focus that spreads from the center to the circumference, as life pours forth freely to life.

TRIUNE COMMUNION AND THE SOCIAL ORDER

There are two points that flow from Scotus's consideration of the Trinity as model for the communal and social sphere. The first has to do with the nature of the family as a distinct embodiment of human society. The second has to do with private property. Both relate to his experience of religious life as framed by the vows of obedience and poverty.

In *Ordinatio* IV, distinction 15, Scotus distinguishes between the family and society. He affirms that the relationship of children to parents is a necessary one, thus belonging to natural law. The obedience children owe to parents is necessitated by the relationship of paternity.[31] Outside the family such obedience is not necessary. However, he writes, one could enter freely into a relationship of obedience where one willingly and freely turns over one's will to another.[32] This sort of act would constitute a type of familial relationship in which one person had authority over another. He offers the political sphere as an example: sometimes peoples come together in freely constituting a political unit. This sort of free allegiance to one another is proper to individuals who are not related to one another, but who seek a union with one another based on a type of contractual understanding.[33] It is also the underlying principle of the vow of obedience in religious orders.

In this same text, Scotus discusses private property and whether or not it is a natural right. Here he argues that in the Garden of Eden prior to the Fall all property was held in common.[34] This was reasonable, since it contributed to a decent way of life and provided all that was needed for survival. No one would have taken what another needed, nor monopolized the goods of the garden. After the Fall, however, things changed. As we saw earlier, the original harmonious relationship of the two internal affections was upset. Concerns for self began to assert themselves as they had not before. Once outside the state of innocence, the human desire to possess became more difficult to control. Peaceful coexistence was threatened; private ownership offered the solution.[35] For this reason, private property may be a reasonable right, even though it is not a natural right. If it were defended as a reasonable right, this would be on the basis of political harmony and peace, since political stability may depend upon a respect for property. A society in which private property is defended may be a more peaceful society than one in which all is held in common. The religious community living according to the more communal sharing of goods (the vow of poverty) would then imitate the state of innocence (or the human community as intended by God).

Clearly, Scotus's early version of a social contract theory and his position on private property can both be read in the context of the religious vows of obedience and poverty. In these two vows we see both the creation of a family-like relationship within a religious order and a life that gives witness to human nature in the state of innocence. Both reflect the life of the Trinity and both, Scotus might argue, offer the conditions for the most fruitful development of the human person as originally intended by God.

CONCLUSIONS

In this chapter we have considered the centrality of the Trinity for Scotus, both as model for the power of love and graciousness and as ideal for human society. In every aspect of his approach, we find the dynamism of a life of love and relationship. That love is the act of divine generosity described by Paul's Letters to the Ephesians, Colossians, and Philippians, and the act of divine presence promised by Jesus at the end of the Gospel of Matthew. In response to divine generosity and presence, the human person is called to a similar life of generosity and presence.

The ultimate communion of each person (and all creation) with God is mediated by the divine act of acceptance, *acceptatio*. This act brings to fruition the first act of creative freedom; it accomplishes the divine order of intention. Scotus views the divine design as relational love. In the human response of love to the created order, understood as gift of a loving Creator, we set in motion the return of all to God. This is not a return that constitutes a long and arduous journey, for just as the father ran out to meet the returning prodigal son, so too Love is racing down time to meet us.

Notes

[1]On the place of the Trinity in Francis's understanding, see Dominic Monti, O.F.M., "Francis as Vernacular Theologian" in *The Franciscan Intellectual Tradition*, Elise Saggau, O.S.F., ed., (St. Bonaventure, NY: Franciscan Institute Publications, 2002), 21-42.

[2]In *Francis and Clare: The Complete Works*, translated with an introduction by Regis Armstrong, O.F.M. and Ignatius Brady, O.F.M., (NY: Paulist Press, 1982), 234.

[3]I am indebted to Henry Beck, O.F.M. for this rich insight.

[4]See *Quodlibet* 16, 379-380, note 23 in *God and Creatures: The Quodlibetal Questions,* Felix Alluntis, Allan B. Wolter, eds., (Princeton, NJ: Princeton University Press, 1975).

[5]This text is translated in *God and Creatures,* 80-107. See Appendix 3, 192-211.

[6]*Quodlibet Question* 4, article 2, 4.46 in *God and Creatures,* 98.

[7]*Quodlibet Question* 4, article 3, 4.68 in *God and Creatures,* 107.

[8]In his discussion of persons in the Trinity, Scotus prefers Richard of St. Victor's definition of person, "the incommunicable existent of an intellectual nature" (*De Trinitate* IV, 21, PL 196: 944-945) to that of Boethius. The traditional Boethian definition of person, "an individual substance of a rational nature" (*De persona et duabis naturis,* PL 64: 1342), when applied to God, results in the unfortunate creation of a fourth person, namely the divine nature or Godhead. See *Ordinatio* I, dist. 23, q.5, 4 (V: 355-356).

[9]*Lectura* I d.2, q.1-4, 164 (16: 166-167). I discuss this presentation in "John Duns Scotus: An Integrated Vision" in *The History of Franciscan Theology,* Kenan Osborne, O.F.M., ed. (St. Bonaventure, NY: The Franciscan Institute 1994), 185-230.

[10]See *Ordinatio* I, d.26, n27-75 (VI: 6-49).

[11]The work of Paul Vignaux has been seminal in regard to the importance of the order of merit and what it reveals about the two freedoms. See in particular his "Lire Duns Scot aujourd'hui" in *Regnum hominis et Regnum Dei,* 33-46 as well as *Justification et predestination au XIVe siècle: Duns Scot, Pierre d'Auriole, Guillaume d'Occam, Grégoire de Rimini* (Paris: Vrin, 1981).

[12]See *Quodlibet* 16 in *God and Creatures,* 16.50, 387.

[13]*Quodlibet Question* 16 focuses on the question of whether or not freedom and necessity can co-exist. See *God and Creatures: The Quodlibetal Questions,* 369-387. See Appendix 3, 192-211.

[14]William A. Frank, "Duns Scotus's Concept of Willing Freely: What Divine Freedom Beyond Choice Teaches Us," *Franciscan Studies* 42 (1982): 86.

[15]I present this example in "Duns Scotus, Morality and Happiness: A Reply to Thomas Williams," *American Catholic Philosophical Quarterly,* 74 (2000): 191-193.

[16]An English version of this text appears as "Duns Scotus on the Necessity of Revealed Knowledge," translated by Allan Wolter, in *Franciscan Studies* 11 (1951): 231-272.

[17]"And so, it is well said that God always rewards beyond our worth, and universally beyond any particular value which an act might merit.

This merit is beyond nature and its intrinsic goodness; it is from a gratuitous divine acceptance. What's more, even beyond that justice which would commonly reward an act, for God rewards by means of pure liberality." *Ordinatio* I, d.17, 149 (5:210). Translation mine.

[18]See *Quodlibet Question* 17 (17.34) in *God and Creatures*, 398.

[19]Scotus states this clearly in *Ordinatio* IV, d.46, in *Duns Scotus on the Will and Morality*, 245. See Appendix 3, 192-211.

[20]Scotus defines theology as *praxis*, not a speculative or contemplative science. See *Ordinatio* Prologue, Pars V (1:55-160).

[21]An English version of this is reproduced in *Duns Scotus on the Will and Morality*, 238-255.

[22]This supports what we said earlier in terms of the *affectio iustitiae* and how it applies to personal dignity and integrity.

[23]"I say that God is no debtor in any unqualified sense save with respect to his own goodness, namely, that he love it. But where creatures are concerned he is debtor rather to his generosity . . ." *Ordinatio* IV, d.46 in *Will and Morality*, 253.

[24]"In an unqualified sense where a creature is concerned, God is just only in relationship to his first justice, namely, because such a creature has been actually willed by the divine will." *Will and Morality*, 255.

[25]I discuss the specific aesthetic dimension of several Scotist texts in "Duns Scotus: Moral Reasoning and the Artistic Paradigm" in *Via Scoti: Methodologica ad Mentem J. Duns Scoti* (Rome: Edizione Antonianum 1995), 825-837. The overall context of merit and divine acceptance is treated in greater depth in *The Harmony of Goodness: Mutuality and Moral Living According to John Duns Scotus* (Quincy, IL: The Franciscan Press, 1996), 117-135.

[26]*Ordinatio* I, d.17, 152 (5:211).

[27]At the close of *Quodlibet Question 17* (*God and Creatures*, 398), Scotus explains the fourfold goodness within the act: voluntary, virtuous, charitable and meritorious. Taken in light of I, d.17, this fourfold goodness could be understood as a four note chord, where each additional level adds to the beauty and richness of the sound. No higher level destroys the lower.

[28]There are clearly Bonaventurian echoes. I would suggest that the only modification Scotus makes to this image is in his emphasis on the free choice to create *ad extra*. This focus on freedom in God reveals his historical situation after the condemnation of 1277.

[29]"In the secret of my heart, teach me wisdom." (Psalm 51:8).

[30]Augustine, *The Confessions* I, 1.

[31]"The first, namely, parental authority, is just by natural law in virtue of which children are bound to obey their parents. Neither was this revoked by any positive Mosaic or Gospel law, but rather it was confirmed." *Ordinatio* IV, d.15, q.2, 7 (Vivès 18: 266) reprinted in *John Duns Scotus: Political and Economic Philosophy* (Allan B. Wolter), Franciscan Institute 2001, 33. See Appendix 3, 192-211.

[32]"Political authority, however, which is exercised over those outside [the family], whether it resides in one person or in a community, can be just by common consent and election on the part of the community. . . . And both of these forms of political authority are just, because one person can justly submit himself to another or to a community in those things which are not against the law of God." Ibid, 33-35.

[33]His insights on this may have been influenced by the Helvetic confederation of states that, in 1291, formed the political entity that is known today as Switzerland. Scotus makes no reference to the Swiss, but it was an event that took place during his early career and could easily have influenced his understanding of a primitive social contract model for political society. Maurice de Gandillac suggests this in "Loi naturelle et fondements de l'ordre social selon les principes du B. Duns Scot" in *De Doctrina I, Duns Scoti* (Rome: Cura Commissionis Scotisticae 1968), II: 706.

[34]"In the state of innocence neither divine or natural law provided for distinct ownership of property; on the contrary everything was common." *Ordinatio* IV, d.15, q.2 in *Political and Economic Philosophy*, 29.

[35]"First of all, communality of all property would have militated against the peaceful life. For the evil and covetous person would take more than needed and, to do so, would also use violence against others who wished to use these common goods for their own needs. . . .Secondly, the original law would also have failed to ensure the necessary sustenance of mankind, for those stronger and more belligerent would have deprived the others of necessities." Ibid., 31.

Chapter 5

Reading Scotus Today

At the conclusion of his short monograph on Thomas Aquinas,[1] Anthony Kenny noted that the value of this thirteenth century Dominican lay not so much in the answers he offered for certain questions, but rather in the questions he raised and the way in which he raised them. In this final chapter, I present a similar argument for John Duns Scotus. Today we witness a renewal of scholarly attention to the work of the Subtle Doctor, both from those unfamiliar with the Franciscan tradition as well as those working within it. This attention originates, in part, from the rebirth of the philosophy of religion, with its attendant reflection upon divine activity and its relationship to human free choice. It is also the result of a more open investigation of medieval thinkers as important figures in the history of philosophy. Today there is a greater appreciation for the richness and diversity of medieval philosopher theologians, both as to the questions they raised and to the methods they followed. Such a context is always good news for Scotus. Indeed, he has stood historically in the shadow of Thomas Aquinas, whose breadth of systematic work far exceeds his own. The Subtle Doctor's *minority* opinion is now of interest to some precisely because it represents an alternate medieval perspective on central human questions. Finally, renewed interest in Scotus arises from an attempt to study more carefully the genesis of modern thought and its pre-modern roots. Here, in particular, the Franciscan holds a prominent place.

Living and teaching at the close of the thirteenth century, Scotus developed two major elements that would become staples of modernity: first, he recast the study of metaphysics as the science of the transcendentals (being, unity, truth, and goodness); second, he focused ethical discussion on the nature of freedom and the contingent world. An appreciation of Scotus's proper place in history depends largely upon how one understands his position on the two central philosophical questions of human knowing and human choice. As I have tried to show in the present study, his perspective on these was framed by his identity as a Franciscan. In other words, Scotus viewed both questions of human knowing and questions of free choice against the background of his theological and spiritual vision of divine nature as loving, Trinitarian communion, of the human person as *imago Dei* and of reality as the unique expression of divine artistic creativity. To these spiritual insights, he brought his own intense and critical intellectual reflection.

Our interest in Scotus goes far beyond his historical significance, however. Indeed, I suggest that one look at Scotist thought not so much for its original answers to questions within the history of medieval philosophy and in our own day; rather, his legacy as a thinker may be found in the important assumptions that lie beneath his arguments. These are the Franciscan assumptions that have formed the organizational pattern for the present study. They are, I would argue, especially apt for our own contemporary situation, at the dawn of the third millennium. In his particular, overall vision of reality and our place within it, Scotus offers more than select answers to isolated questions; he challenges us to consider carefully the deeper positions we take for granted.

In this challenge, Scotus finds us willing to question the assumptions of modernity. Indeed, contemporary reflection (both philosophical and theological) recognizes its limits and searches for other ways of understanding human existence and its relationship to the divine. In philosophy, the conceptual frame of modernity, dominant since the seventeenth century and informed by the assumptions of the enlightenment, has been superceded in this so-called *postmodern*[2] era of deconstructionism. In science, the twentieth century revolution of quantum physics has called into question the enlightenment models of nature, objectivity and rationality. Spiritual yearnings express themselves in the growth and development of New Age approaches. In the concrete order, technology now dominates societies, threatening the traditional understanding of human dignity and value. In economy, increased globalization results in the growing disparity between rich and poor. In this moment we cast about for other ways of seeing our reality, hoping to find conceptual models to help integrate a world that has become too complex, too fragmented for us to bear. In particular, we are in need of a new philosophical anthropology, a new vision of what it means to be human.

Medieval thinkers like Scotus can be a rich resource for us. By examining more closely their intellectual legacy, we discover principles to help us integrate the scientific with the religious, the intellectual with the spiritual. They can help us *precisely* insofar as they were religious and spiritual thinkers who saw the world in which they lived as a coherent whole, one whose secrets were accessible to, but not exhausted by, human reflection. In their attempt to understand and explain the phenomena and their own experiences, such thinkers were optimistic without being naïve. They recognized the limits of human rationality, and explained these limits in terms of our present condition (the *status iste*), subsequent to the fall. Nonetheless, attentive to a deeper awareness of the beauty of the whole, they examined reality with a critical eye. In Scotus's Franciscan perspective, we discover those scientific, intellectual, and spiritual aspects that constitute an aesthetic vision of value, framed around rational love as the highest expression of human nature. This vision of reality ennobles the human mind and spirit, calling upon the rational human desire for and love of the good. With the centrality of beauty, Franciscans like Scotus offer a particular way of understanding the human person, the nature of God, the value of creation and the relationship of all these to one another. This way of understanding is founded upon love, beauty, and freedom as expressions of rationality, both divine and human. All three are located in the will, seat of desire and choice. The human activity of imitating God is best identified in our response to the good that appears as the beautiful. In loving what is good, the human heart most nobly reflects divine creative activity.

The coherence of Scotus's intellectual insights (both philosophical and theological) stem from his spiritual vision *precisely* insofar as he is Franciscan writing after the Condemnation of 1277.[3] Indeed, the Franciscan spiritual and intellectual tradition of the late thirteenth century informs his commitment to divine freedom and the importance of the contingent order. It supports his reflection upon the dignity of the human person as *imago Christi*. Finally, it sustains his moral aesthetic as a spiritual participation in the rational order of love that creates and sustains all that is. These three dimensions of Scotist thought: the defense of freedom, the affirmation of human dignity, and the centrality of beauty as a moral category all provide fruitful ways to reconsider contemporary assumptions about what it means to be human, what it means to be rational, and what it means to participate in divine life. The human journey for Scotus is, ultimately, an intellectual-spiritual journey founded upon the recognition and experience of beauty. This recognition leads to the discovery of divine artistic freedom and love as the source of what exists. This discovery, finally, gives birth to the human desire to respond freely with a love that is both gratitude and charity.

THE DEFENSE OF FREEDOM

In "John Duns Scotus in the Postmodern, Scientific World,"[4] Kenan Osborne, O.F.M., highlights two central characteristics of our contemporary society: first, our obsession with technology and science; and second, our anti-religious secularism. Both of these, he argues, point to the deeper rift between the domains of scientific knowledge and spirituality, of reason and faith. As a result, contemporary society is rationally fragmented; our ability to live a fully human life is thereby endangered. Both of these characteristics support a defense of human autonomy understood as an exercise of freedom independent from God.

The deification of science and the exaltation of anti-religious secularism belong to the modern ambivalence toward transcendence. On the one hand, the last four hundred years of modernity have sought the absolute knowledge that science offered. On the other hand, this same era has been suspicious of any dimension that might threaten human autonomy. Accordingly, divine existence and divine freedom threaten the fullest expression of human freedom and human existence; divine power threatens the fullest realization of human gifts. The enlightenment project to keep a healthy distance between divine and human worlds relied upon a *particular* understanding of the nature of scientific knowledge and upon a *particular* understanding of the nature of God. The first has been called into question by the scientific revolution and the advent of postmodernity. The second is in the process of revision.

Both contingency and perspectivism figure prominently in contemporary scientific theories and in the philosophical discourse of postmodernity.[5] In its critical realism, Scotist thought embraces and transcends the value of contingency with the affirmation of the need for multiple perspectives, each grounded in reality outside the mind (made possible with the formal distinction). Scotus can be a dialogue partner for such a time and, thankfully, one who sees beyond the many perspectives to a greater whole, defined by beauty. He contextualizes his affirmation of the radical contingency of the created order within a vision of divine love and artistic freedom. Reality is shot through with contingency, from the first moment of divine choice to create this order to the smallest exercise of human free willing. Such contingency is neither random nor arbitrary. Rather, there is an explanation for the order of things, an explanation ultimately reducible to the divine nature as rational, loving presence. Unless we understand the divine nature that stands behind Scotus's reflection on freedom, we can too easily misread his assertions regarding the nature of created world, the human exercise of freedom and the presence of God as sustaining cause for all that exists.

Scotus's defense of freedom (both in the divine and human wills) throughout his teaching career was a defense of the superiority of liberality and generosity over necessity and obligation. It was the affirmation of the value of love and mercy over the requirements of justice. The ability of the divine will to choose to create this world from all the possible worlds open to divine creativity reveals the value and dignity of the present, contingent order as expression of divine desire that is intentional and purposeful. And, so as to insure the possibility of human action as image of divine, the very freedom enjoyed by God at the moment of creation belongs to the human will, albeit in a limited version.

This means that human freedom, in its fullest expression, imitates and reveals the nature of divine freedom as rational, creative love. God's ability to choose is mirrored by our own ability to make choices, to control our own desires, to refrain from action where needed. Just as nothing outside the divine nature is such that it ever compels or necessitates the divine will, so too nothing outside the human person is so compelling that it determines choices. External circumstances can influence human choice, to be sure, but human freedom is naturally constituted as rational and capable of independent movement. This rational constitution of human freedom enhances our exercise of choice and makes those moments of moral decision unique expressions of character. Our actions, like God's actions, flow from our integrity and are ultimately measured against our personal identity. To act with integrity belongs to the highest expression of rational freedom. To act in this way out of love is to participate in divine life.

Scotus's defense of freedom as part of the will's rational constitution belongs also to his conviction that true human conversion, whether moral or religious, is always possible. The ability of an individual to turn her life around, to move in another, better direction, to stop harmful or destructive behavior depends upon a moment of self-control, where the person is (as it were) immobile in the presence of external circumstances. Like the dancer, at this moment the person is poised to act. Here is the still point, the center of rational action, that exquisitely brief moment of self-awareness and self-possession. The will's indeterminacy, its independence from external factors is the logical requirement for any self-movement, any change of direction that belongs to the individual alone. The existence and defense of such a level of personal autonomy constitute the basis upon which we give any praise or blame.

The two aspects of Scotus's defense of freedom, the ability for independent action (indeterminacy) and the fullness of rational integrity (self-determinacy), belong to the divine and human wills. In the divine will, clearly, these exist at the fullest level of perfection according to the divine nature. Their exercise constitutes value. In the human will, these aspects are proper to our nature. Their exercise does not constitute value, but is measured by value. When we act in imitation of God, we bring together both indeterminacy and self-determinacy in the way that the fully formed artist is in full and complete control of his actions. To act with the integrity of freedom is to act in imitation of the divine Artist whose rational creativity brings forth order out of chaos, beauty out of nothing.

So, while Scotus defends human rational freedom in a manner that is very attractive to contemporary discussion, he never separates the exercise of human free choice from its exemplar in the divine will. In addition, the exercise of human free choice is continually supported by the divine will in its loving presence. For Scotus, human and divine wills are not at odds with one another, because human and divine love are not at odds. The natural human desire to love the good for itself alone is ultimately perfected in love for God. As Augustine's *Confessions* illustrates so clearly, the exercise of human loving, even when misdirected, is part of the rational road to the discovery of the divine.

THE AFFIRMATION OF HUMAN DIGNITY

As we have seen, Scotus continually affirms and defends the dignity of the human person. His teaching on *haecceitas* points to the unique character of each individual, of each being. His position on the Incarnation and Immaculate Conception reveal the fundamental insight of the value of human nature and of each human person. His optimistic philosophical anthropology brings together love, rationality and freedom to frame his reflection upon the human condition and human journey from this world to God. Scotus never hesitates to attribute perfection to human nature, so long as Scripture and right reasoning are not in opposition. Among these attributes are the power of the human intellect, the superiority of the rational will and the exercise of human love.

While, for Scotus, the intellect is not the rational potency, cognition clearly plays a central role in the human journey to God. To that end, the intellect enjoys two cognitive activities: abstraction and intuition. Through both, the person is able to know the truth about God and, more importantly, see God face to face in the beatific vision. The fullness of human happiness, eternal life, is not foreign to the constitution of our nature, as intended by God. In heaven, we need no additional light of glory, nor additional divine help, to exercise the natural gifts we have been given. Rather, heaven becomes the experience where the human person can fully exercise all she naturally possesses, in direct communion with God.

Intellectual activity (through abstractive and intuitive cognition) is essential to the human moral journey as well. Because Scotus endows the will with such an important exercise of rational, autonomous freedom, he can endow the intellect as well with a stronger cognitive activity. Right reasoning (the activity of the intellect in prudential judgment) can conclude with the highest possible certainty about what course of action to take in a given situation. At no time, however, does this conclusion compel or necessitate the cooperation of the will.

The distinction between intuitive and abstractive acts of the intellect allows Scotus to reconcile the Aristotelian (and philosophical) position on human knowing with the Augustinian (and theological) position. The Franciscan understands the philosophical position on abstraction as more proper to the human intellect in this life (our *status iste*), as part of the consequences of sin and not as a result of our nature as embodied beings. The theological position on intuition, for its part, better describes human nature and is proper to the intellect in the life to come. Both are part of our experience, however, with intuition having more to do with our subjective states of self-awareness and memory. The intuitive act is key to repentance and conversion.

Together, the two acts support the affirmation of human dignity by allowing for the highest form of scientific knowledge of this world and in this life (abstraction), and for another, higher act of understanding in the life to come (intuition). In addition, it is from the perspective of intuition that human understanding in this world can be critiqued. The limits of human knowing can only be recognized from a point that lies beyond them. In this way, Scotist thought is both critical of human cognition (in a way that joins modern philosophical reflection) and transcends that critique (in a way that is attractive to the postmodern concerns). Scotus transcends the critique, however, as a theologian. Once again, the convergence of intellectual and spiritual insights offers another way to understand the human person as both limited and capable of transcending limitation.

One of the most challenging aspects of Scotus's vision of the human person is his position on rational love. Indeed, today one hardly thinks of love as rational at all. We see the intellect as seat of rationality. We more easily attribute to love the emotional, passionate, and uncontrollable energies that belong to the human heart. In his discussion of the most basic human desires, Scotus offers another lens through which we might understand ourselves and our deepest fulfillment.

The two affections on the will (the affection for justice and the affection for possession) are the rational foundations for Scotus's affirmation of the centrality of love and defense of the existence of freedom. These two affections bring together rationality and love as central to the constitution of the human person. Through them, Scotus shows how the fullest perfection of the human person as rational is realized by right and ordered loving.[6]

Further reflection upon these two affections, not lost through original sin, is needed today. Together they reconcile the concerns for the self (affection for possession), that are healthy and necessary for human perfection, with the concerns for the other and for those goods of value (affection for justice) that are required for the fullness of a happy life. Together they explain how rational self-control is the heart of human freedom and how in our everyday choices we should be concerned to have the proper balance between concerns for value and concerns for the self. As Scotus explains the exercise of human free choice as rational loving, the demands of value always inform and enlighten the natural desire for self-protection. It is when these two affections are not in harmony, when one exerts undue influence over the other, that human behavior is unhealthy, irrational and, ultimately, not free. When they are in harmony, we imitate God in whom love for the highest good and love for the self coincide.

The human natural ability to love the highest good in itself and for itself alone is the foundation for the human act of love for God, defended by Scotus as a natural act. This means that all persons, by virtue of their rational constitution (i.e., the two affections) are capable of loving God above all things *naturally*. No grace is needed for any one person to love God. Human nature is thus so constituted with the natural dignity of love for the good. This natural constitution of the human will was not wounded by the fall, as was the human intellect. Indeed, human nature was made in this way for the purpose of the Incarnation, so that our nature would be capable of receiving such a great gift as the divine presence, not simply to us but, more importantly, with us.

BEAUTY AS A MORAL CATEGORY

Finally, Scotist thought challenges our modern sensibilities in the way he brings together love, rationality and freedom in an aesthetic vision of the whole. Beauty finalizes the human experience of rationality. It is divine beauty that continues to inspire and inform the human journey of love. Beauty offers us the best vantage point from which to reflect upon the God who has brought us into being, and to imitate this God in our daily actions.

The centrality of beauty in Scotist thought should not be reduced to a subjective experience of individual enjoyment. Rather, like Augustine and Bonaventure before him, Scotus draws upon the Platonic and Neoplatonic traditions that saw beauty as an objective reality whose constitution can be rationally analyzed without losing the dynamic of attraction and love. Divine beauty draws and fulfills human longing, integrates human desire and rational choice. In the recognition of divine beauty and its affect upon us, we see again the unity of the will's two affections. In recognizing the highest good as beauty, we experience the highest delight and gratitude. In the experience of beauty, the intellect and will are brought into a single act of loving presence.

To understand God as ultimate Beauty and as ultimate Artist is to grasp the human vocation to be artists and creators of beauty. In our moral lives, we bring forth beauty in imitation of divine creative artistic activity.[7]

RATIONAL LOVE: THE FRANCISCAN ALTERNATIVE

Richard Rohr, a contemporary Franciscan, reflects upon his experience within our modern culture as an age of anxiety.[8] He suggests that the Franciscan tradition may have an alternative to offer to this present situation. Rohr points to an overall loss of meaning, stemming from the scientific recognition that the universe is radically contingent. He notes that the rejection of scientific objectivity has removed any rational moorings from contemporary reflection, especially moral reflection. Once the rational moorings have been removed, then any claim to moral objectivity is tenuous at best. Often moral reflection is reduced to sincerity or emotions as the only basis upon which to defend one's actions. As we know, sincerity is no substitute for moral reflection, nor do feelings always adequately reflect what should be done in a given situation.

The situation described by Rohr is critical. Some understand it as the failure of the enlightenment project. In this present work, I have tried to suggest that Scotus, as a representative of the Franciscan tradition, does indeed have a coherent and well-framed response to many of the concerns of our own day. It is, I would argue, a viable alternative to the enlightenment project that does not sacrifice many of the key values of that endeavor:

the affirmation of human dignity, the importance of rational reflection, the centrality of freedom and autonomy. Scotus's vision also brings with it an optimism about the human journey and the created order. He readily acknowledges the contingent order as the result of divine free choice. His is a theological vision not focused on sin or fallenness. His is a reflection upon divine perfection not in terms of absolute power but in terms of limitless love.[9] Finally, his is a description of human fulfillment that unites intellectual and spiritual aspirations.

With this vision, Scotus offers a better response to the present state of human anxiety than does either modern or postmodern thought. This is the case because Scotus's assumptions are quite different than either of the two dominant philosophical visions today. Modernity and postmodernity share a common assumption in their vision of what it means to be human. This vision is fragmented both internally and interpersonally. It is fragmented internally, first, insofar as it sets spiritual aspirations against intellectual desire. For both, it is intellectual rather than spiritual activity that defines rationality. Indeed, spiritual activity lies, practically by definition, beyond reason. Accordingly, religion deals with what we cannot understand. This sort of conclusion springs from a too-secularized vision of human reason. This secularized vision does not identify the intellect as a spiritual faculty. It sees human knowing as unrelated to religious or spiritual development. Indeed, the two are polar opposites. Additionally, this vision is fragmented interpersonally insofar as it is focused on the individual as a non-relational being. Adulthood is defined by a notion of the autonomous individual as radically free and independent of others. To be an adult means to be able to make one's own decisions. To be an individual also means to have certain rights that must be respected by others. Relationships, commitment, and communitarian goods have not played a prominent role in this vision of the human person.

Postmodernist philosophers attempt to overcome the binary, either/or approach of modernity. However, because postmodern thinkers too often share the basic assumptions of modernity about what it means to be rational, in their response they struggle with the issue of transcendence, either for scientific knowledge or for knowledge of God.[10] Thus, in rejecting the absolutism of science, postmodernism can too easily reject any higher dimension accessible to human reason and reflection.[11] All perspectives are equal and equally horizontal. The result here, of course, is either nihilism (for the agnostic) or mysticism (for the believer). In either case, however, language fails the human desire for understanding or meaning. This failure of language is critical, since all reflection becomes merely subjective projection of inner need, with no objective meaning beyond individual, personal preferences. While postmodernism attempts to solve the problems of modernity, it has not yet realized that in order to do so it must re-think even its own assumptions.

Both modernity and postmodernity agree that the term *rationality* refers to intellectual activity. In addition, both explain knowing in terms of representational thinking.[12] While modernity sought to establish itself on the basis of a certainty that goes beyond possible deception, postmodernity rejects certainty altogether, turning to the subjectivity proper to a single individual. Some postmodern thinkers have, to a great extent, accepted the terms of the representational model of modernity and concluded from it that, given the primacy of subjective desires and psychological states, no such thing as truth can ever be asserted. Indeed, truth is personal and private, if it exists at all. Any statement is only a perspective, only an opinion; nothing is true or false. Our minds are disconnected from the world outside ourselves in a radical way: indeed, I may be dreaming right now and you may not exist at all. Conversely, you may be dreaming right now and I may not exist at all. Or, we might be part of a dream that someone else is having.

Finally, both modernity and postmodernity accept the notion of freedom as radical indeterminacy, unrelated to rationality (that is, to the intellect). Freedom is located in the will alone; it is a personal ability to choose and to choose independently of anyone else. I am freer when I have more options. Since we cannot know anything as it is in itself, then freedom has no objective grounding, it becomes the ability to do whatever we want, not because we know it is good but because we want it. In our democratic societies we are experiencing the negative fallout from this, for once freedom is separated from rationality, anything goes. Nobody can tell anyone else what to do, what should be done, or why something is right or wrong. Here again, this is where rights enter in, and the discussion can turn to a power struggle.

This time in history might be Scotus's time. As we have seen in each of the chapters, Scotus has an answer to these assumptions. It is for this reason that I consider Duns Scotus to be an enormously important thinker for today. In the guise of a conclusion, then, I now lay out this answer very briefly.

First, Scotus's anthropology is unbelievably optimistic. While he accepts the notion of a fall, of original sin, he works to limit its effects as much as possible. Human nature is not fallen in a radical sense; however, it is wounded. Even so, we have not lost the affection for justice. Indeed, it is what constitutes our freedom as rational beings. Its harmonious relationship to the affection for possession is nonetheless skewed. One must work harder, put in a bit more effort, to achieve that preternatural harmony intended by God. This means that each person (believer or nonbeliever) has all the rational gifts necessary both to know and to love God in this life. Human nature also has all the rational gifts necessary to experience the beatific vision. In heaven, there will be no need for a supernatural light of glory, as Thomas Aquinas maintained, in order to know and love God.

Second, Scotus shifts the center of his vision from sinfulness to the primacy of Christ. As we have seen, his explanation for the Incarnation is completely independent of human sinfulness. Had Adam and Eve never sinned, he argues, God would still have become flesh because of the value and dignity with which human persons were created. Indeed, the Incarnation was the purpose of creation. According to Scotus, God intends to share divine life in communion with every single human person. In order to do this, there must be a person who *is* that very communion, that is, a person who unites two natures in one person. This person is Jesus. As a result of this shift toward the Incarnation, Scotus defends the Immaculate Conception of Mary. Here again, Scotus both separates original sin from human sexuality and explains how it is that someone who has not sinned still needs salvation.

We come, finally, to the most optimistic aspect of Scotus's vision: the way he continually exalts rational freedom, not in terms of its limitless options or even in terms of individual autonomy, but as generosity and liberality, both in God and (potentially) in us. According to Scotus's vision of the human journey toward God, all that has been created by God has been created out of love. It is divine love that sustains and guides all beings toward the ultimate experience of communion.

In Scotus's discussion of freedom and the generous liberality of divine and human goodness, he regularly returns to examples taken from art and from artistic creativity: the artist, the artisan, the musician, the lute-player. God is understood as the artist whose creative activity is radically free in the way an artist is radically free (but not arbitrary or random) in the creation of the work of art. In this radical freedom of artistic creativity, we can still count on artistic integrity: that dimension of divine life (love) that will remain constant and steadfast, whatever the response. In addition, God is also presented by Scotus as the delighted listener of the music performed by the created order and, indeed, by the human heart. When we love in an ordered way, not guided by our own personal needs and desires alone but guided by our understanding of what the situation or person needs, then God is pleased. When we do this out of love for God, God's response is delight. Scotus likens God to the listener of music, delighted by the harmony of the performance and particularly delighted by the intention of the performer, who is bringing all his best gifts to bear on this singular moment in time and doing it out of love.

In his response to the contemporary scene, as described by Richard Rohr, Scotus would argue that one can have a contingent cosmos and still affirm order in reality. That is, the rejection of meaning does not necessarily follow from the affirmation of contingency. In Scotus's vision, the universe is radically contingent in all its parts, in the relationship of the parts, in the foundational laws that apply to it, and in its first moment of existence. Because he connects all these to the divine loving act of generous artistic freedom, he can agree with contemporary scientists that chaos theory may be a more appropriate description of reality and still argue for the order of all that exists. Indeed, Scotus argues that nothing exists in a vacuum; everything is ordered to everything else. All reality is relational, and by divine design.

In addition, Scotus would point out that, thanks to the intuitive act of cognition, the human mind has some non-representational access to the extra-mental world. This immediacy is not complete knowing, nor is it understanding of the true and complete nature of things. It is, however, the foundational bridge that is required to escape the critique of modernity and postmodernity that offers only one, representational model[13] and charges human knowing with a radical separation from the world around it. Intuitive cognition avoids the critique leveled against this model of knowing, where any image is capable of deception.

Finally, Scotist thought offers the objective order of value based upon an absolute moral first principle: God is to be loved. This first principle is self-evident and analytic in its truth. Since God is the highest and most perfect good, then God is worthy of love above all things, and for God alone. This statement has a truth that is immediately known and is, itself, the ground for all other moral truths. As Scotus explains, the commands of the Ten Commandments are themselves the expression of divine desire and reveal God's will in our lives. They are not absolute in the sense that the first command is absolute, but they do express the relationship we should have with the neighbor out of love for God. In this way, Scotus calls our attention to the commandments without making all moral living obligational in nature. Indeed, our desire to love rightly is perfected when we love as God loves. Any act of right loving strengthens our relationship with one another and with God. Scripture completes what human reason knows to be true. The domains of faith and reason are, therefore, not at odds, but work to complement one another.

Human love, rightly understood as rational and as free, best fulfills the human desire for happiness. The two affections of the human will, the affection for justice and for possession, are both fulfilled in the completely moral act. When I act justly, I am most happy. This is what we will know in heaven, when love for the highest good (God) will complete our human desire for satisfaction. Pleasure, power and random action, then, do not fulfill the deepest longing of the human heart. Right loving, integrity and generosity do.

FINAL REFLECTIONS

In my own case, Scotus offered a series of interesting philosophical insights until I recognized the spiritual point behind it all. I had struggled for years to make sense of ideas that were, as far as I was concerned, interesting yet disconnected, if not at odds with one another. Then, one day, it all fell into place. That was the day I recognized the centrality of beauty for him as a Franciscan, along with the role of love and creativity. Creativity, love and beauty are the foundation of his intellectual vision because he belongs to the particular spiritual tradition he does. I find that where scholars misread or misunderstand Scotus they have not taken adequate account of his spiritual vision precisely as a Franciscan. This vision is grounded on the power of ordered loving as central to a correct understanding of human nature as rational; on the Trinity as model both for reality and for human relationships; and on an aesthetic perspective that is the basis for his discussion of moral goodness.

I have come to the conclusion that Scotus's philosophical insights cannot easily be separated from his theological preoccupation, nor should they be. Here is a thinker who is consciously spiritual in his intellectual endeavor and consciously Christian in his understanding of the divine nature, without dismissing the value of insights that come from other non-Christian perspectives. The God of Scotus is the God of John 3:16, who so loved the world he gave his only Son; the God of Paul's letter to the Ephesians 1: 4-6, who predestines all to glory; the God of Matthew 20, the Master who rewards workers far beyond what they deserve and wonders why some grumble because he is generous. Here is a notion of divine justice interpreted in terms of divine mercy and liberality, not in terms of a strict understanding of giving what is due. The God of Scotus is the God of Francis of Assisi, a God so generous he throws everything away out of love. This may be the very God our world so needs today.

Historically, there exists a tension within the Franciscan tradition between the intellectual and the spiritual. With his concept of rationality as ordered loving, Scotus offers a way in which one might understand this tension as creative, insofar as it suggests a renewed and more integrated way to understand the human person as both scientist and artist, philosopher and poet, a person of rational faith. Because, for Scotus, the aesthetic is more basic than the scientific, intellectual activity is integrated within a broader context defined not by knowing but by loving.

Generosity and love establish the basis for Scotus's discussion of the Incarnation. With him, we enter a Christocentric vision of salvation considered independently of human sinfulness. Our categories of soteriology change from those of justice to generosity and, more importantly, focus on the divine desire to be present with us. Divine delight becomes a category within which we consider creation and the value of each being as pleasing to God (a metaphysical consideration). Within such a perspective we understand the motivation both behind the covenant with the People of Israel and in the Incarnation (a theological insight); from this appreciation, finally, we anticipate the glory that awaits us and how we might participate in divine life by imitating divine creativity (the moral perspective).

No scholar of Thomas Aquinas would ever dare study his work without some awareness of Aristotelian philosophy, nor of some sense of what Thomas thought about Aristotle. No reputable scholar of Bonaventure is unfamiliar with Platonic thought and its Augustinian transmission to the Middle Ages. Likewise, those who approach Scotus should consider the implications of his Franciscan identity as well as the influence of his spiritual tradition on his writings. I am increasingly convinced that much of the language Scotus speaks is informed by his spiritual and religious assumptions. A contemporary scholar with no sense of the Franciscan vision may miss what is really going on behind such arguments. If those who live within the tradition of religious or Franciscan life do not enter the conversation at the scholarly level, our colleagues cannot be blamed for missing the point. It is important to find ways to make the Franciscan spiritual argument an integral part of the larger scholarly and intellectual conversation. This is really to say that it is important to engage spiritual insights in the birthing of a new vision of the human, one in which the spiritual and rational are better integrated.

Anyone familiar with history is aware of the enormous transitions that were going on at the time of Francis of Assisi: the intellectual and scientific revolution of Aristotelian philosophy; the rise of the middle class; the crusades and religious animosity among Christians, Jews, and Moslems at the political and international level; the scandals of Church leadership; the increasing gap between rich and poor. Francis and the important thinkers who belonged to the Franciscan intellectual tradition (men like Alexander of Hales and Bonaventure) brought to that time a particular vision of what it means to be human, to be a follower of Jesus. Their intellectual vision was inclusive and aesthetic, grounded upon their Christian recognition of divine bountiful goodness and the beauty of the created order.

In our own time, we find ourselves at similar historical crossroads. We too have seen the scientific revolution of quantum mechanics and chaos theory, we too have seen the spread of market-driven capitalism throughout the world, we too see the Middle East as the place of conflict among the members of three major western world religions – and we have seen the tragedy of September 11, 2001. We, too, are scandalized by the actions of ordained clergy and Church leaders; we, too, witness the increasing gap between rich and poor due to the unbelievable misuse of the goods of the earth by only a fraction of its inhabitants. Indeed, the era of the thirteenth and fourteenth centuries shares much with the dawning of the third millennium.

The question that faces all Christians today is the question before us: what resources do our own spiritual and intellectual traditions offer to help us address the contemporary crisis? Can we be a prophetic and counter-cultural voice in the face of a secularized, technologically advanced world that progresses at the expense of the most vulnerable? Can we work to change not

just the structures of injustice but also the structures of thinking that support and justify the injustice? In his intellectual
and spiritual vision of reality, Scotus may offer the resources of
the Franciscan and Christian tradition to address in a coherent
way the needs of all. His thought may be another support for
rebuilding not just the Church but also an entire society, indeed, the entire world.

We face a contemporary world that is so deeply broken that
God can look upon it only as Jesus looked upon the crowds, like
sheep without a shepherd. As Francis responded to the needs of
his time and to the call to rebuild the church so, too, are we
called upon to respond to the needs of our time and help rebuild
a broken world. With the help of the intellectual legacy of Duns
Scotus (and others) we may be able to play our part in the divine desire to bring all things together, in and through Christ
Jesus. In this effort, the Subtle Doctor may indeed be a thinker
whose time has, once again, come.

Notes

[1]*Aquinas,* Past Masters Series (Oxford: Oxford University Press,
1980), 81.

[2]I use this term only for convenience. It is the case that several
contemporary thinkers are not sympathetic to this way of describing
them or their work.

[3]This important historical event had a significant influence upon how
thinkers in the final quarter of the thirteenth century approached
Aristotelian thought, understood the relationship of philosophy to
theology and considered key human questions. See above, chapter 1.

[4]*The Franciscan Intellectual Tradition*, Elise Saggau, O.S.F., ed. (St.
Bonaventure, NY: Franciscan Institute Publications, 2002), 57-82.

[5]See for example François Lyotard, *The Postmodern Condition: A
Report on Knowledge*, trans. Geoff Bennington and Brian Massumi
(Minneapolis: University of Minnesota Press, 1984); Jacques Derrida,
Of Grammatology, trans. G. C. Spivak (Baltimore: Johns Hopkins
University Press, 1976); and more recently, Jacques Derrida,

Circumfession, trans. Geoff Bennington (Chicago: University of Chicago Press, 1993).

[6]Emmanuel Levinas develops the theme of love for the neighbor as the most proper way for the person to relate to God. See his *Entre Nous: Thinking-of-the-Other*, trans. Smith/Harshav (New York: Columbia University Press, 1998), 103.

[7]I develop this in greater detail in *The Harmony of Goodness: Mutuality and Moral Living According to John Duns Scotus* (Quincy: Franciscan Press, 1996).

[8]*Hope Against Darkness: The Transforming Vision of Saint Francis in an Age of Anxiety* (Cincinnati: St. Anthony Messenger Press, 2001).

[9]The emphasis on divine love rather than divine power has parallels in Richard Kearney, *The God Who May Be: A Hermeneutics of Religion* (Bloomington: Indiana University Press, 2001).

[10]For example, Richard Kearney (see note 9) attempts a "poetics of religion" in an attempt to overcome a purely horizontal perspective.

[11]While most postmodern thinkers are suspicious of transcendent knowledge there is great concern regarding transcendence. See for example, Jean-Luc Marion, *God Without Being*, trans. Thomas A. Carleson (Chicago: University of Chicago Press, 1991); *God, the Gift and Postmodernism*, eds. J. Caputo and M. Scanlon (Bloomington: Indiana University Press, 1999) and *Questioning God*, eds. J. Caputo and M. Scanlon (Bloomington: Indiana University Press, 2001).

[12]The best example would be Levinas's reaction against Husserl and Heidegger. Much of contemporary postmodern discourse on God and religion takes Levinas's reaction as more or less justified. The post-Levinasian view of reason tends to characterize it as a grasping, representational kind of thinking.

[13]Kearney's poetics might be an atypical attempt. See note 9 above.

Appendix One

Reading One
Chapter III of *De Primo Principio*, 3.3-3.22.
First Proof for God's Existence[1]

3.1 The triple primacy of the First Principle.

3.2 O Lord, our God, you have proclaimed yourself to be the first and last. Teach your servant to show by reason what he holds with faith most certain, that you are the most eminent, the first efficient cause and the last end.

3.3 We would like to select three of the six essential orders referred to earlier, the two of extrinsic causality and the one of eminence and, if you grant us to do so, to demonstrate that in these three orders there is some one nature which is simply first. I say one "nature" advisedly, since in this third chapter these three ways of being first will be shown to characterize not a unique singular or what is but one in number, but a unique essence or nature. Numerical unity, however, will be discussed later.

3.4 (First conclusion) *Some nature among beings can produce an effect.*

3.5 This is shown to be so because something can be produced and therefore something can be productive. The implication is evident from the nature of correlatives. Proof of the antecedent: (1) Some nature is contingent. It is possible for it to exist after being nonexistent, not of itself, however, or by reason of nothing, for in both these cases a being would exist by reason of what is not a being. Therefore it is producible by another. (2) Some nature too is changeable or mobile, since it can lack some perfection it is able to have. The result of the change then can begin to be and thus be produced.

3.6 In this conclusion, as in some of those which follow, I could argue in terms of the actual thus. Some nature is producing since some nature is produced, because some nature begins to exist, for some nature is contingent and the result of motion. But I prefer to propose conclusions and premises about the possible. For once those about the actual are granted, those about the possible are also conceded, but the reverse is not the case. Also those about the actual are contingent, though evident enough, whereas those about the possible are necessary. The former concern the being as existing whereas the latter can pertain properly to a being considered even in terms of its essentials. The existence of this essence, of which efficiency is now established, will be proved later.

3.7 (Second conclusion) *Something able to produce an effect is simply first, that is to say, it neither can be produced by an efficient cause nor does it exercise its efficient causality in virtue of anything other than itself.*

3.8 It is proved from the first conclusion that something can produce an effect. Call this producer A. If A is first in the way explained, we have immediately what we seek to prove. If it is not such, then it is a posterior agent either because it can be produced by something else or because it is able to produce its effect only in virtue of some agent other than itself. To deny the negation is to assert the affirmation. Let us assume that this being is not first and call it B. Then we can argue of B as we did of A. Either we go on *ad infinitum* so that each thing in reference to what precedes it in the series will be second; or we shall reach something that has nothing prior to it. However, an infinity in the ascending order is impossible; hence a primacy is necessary because whatever has nothing prior is not posterior to anything posterior to itself, for the second conclusion of chapter two does away with a circle in causes.

3.9 An objection is raised here on the grounds that those who philosophize admit that an infinity is possible in an ascending order, as they themselves were wont to assume infinite generators of which none is first but each is second to some other, and still they assume no circle in causes. In ruling out this objection I declare that the philosophers did not postulate the possibility of an infinity in causes essentially ordered but only in causes accidentally ordered, as is evident from Avicenna's *Metaphysics*, B. VI, chapter five, where he speaks of an infinity of individuals in a species.

3.10 But to show what I have in mind, I will explain what essentially ordered and accidentally ordered causes are. Here recall that it is one thing to speak of incidental causes (*causae per accidens*) as contrasted with those which are intended to cause a given effect (*causae per se*). It is quite another to speak of causes which are ordered to one another essentially or of themselves (*per se*) and those which are ordered only accidentally (*per accidens*).

For in the first instance, we have merely a one-to-one comparison, [namely] of the cause to that which is caused. A *per se* cause is one which causes a given effect by reason of its proper nature and not in virtue of something incidental to it. In the second instance, two causes are compared with each other insofar as they are causes of the same thing.

3.11 *Per se* or essentially ordered causes differ from accidentally ordered causes in three respects. The first difference is that in essentially ordered causes, the second depends upon the first precisely in the act of causing. In accidentally ordered causes this is not the case, although the second may depend upon the first for its existence or in some other way. The second difference is that in essentially ordered causes the causality is of another nature and order, inasmuch as the higher cause is the more perfect, which is not the case with accidentally ordered causes. This second difference is a consequence of the first, since no cause in the exercise of its causality is essentially dependent upon a cause of the same nature as itself, for to produce anything one cause of a given kind suffices. A third difference follows, viz. that all essentially ordered causes are simultaneously required to cause the effect, for otherwise some causality essential to the effect would be wanting. In accidentally ordered causes this simultaneity is not required.

3.12 What we intend to show from this is that an infinity, of essentially ordered causes is impossible, and that an infinity of accidentally ordered causes is also impossible unless we admit a *terminus* in an essentially ordered series. Therefore there is no way in which an infinity in essentially ordered causes is possible. And even if we deny the existence of an essential order, an infinity of causes is still impossible. Consequently in any case there is something able to produce an effect which is simply first. Here three propositions are assumed. For the sake of brevity, call the first A, the second B and the third C.

3.13 The proof of these: first, A is proved. (1) If the totality of essentially ordered causes were caused, it would have to be by a cause which does not belong to the group, otherwise it would be its own cause. The whole series of dependents then is dependent and upon something which is not one of the group. (2) [If this were not so], an infinity of essentially ordered causes would be acting at the same time (a consequence of the third difference mentioned above). Now no philosopher assumes this. (3) Thirdly, to be prior, according to Bk. V of the *Metaphysics*, a thing must be nearer the beginning. Consequently, where there is no beginning, nothing can be essentially prior to anything else. (4) Fourthly, by reason of the second difference, the higher cause is more perfect in its causality, therefore what is infinitely higher is infinitely more perfect, and hence of infinite perfection in its causing. Therefore it does not cause in virtue of another, because everything of this kind is imperfect in its causality, since it depends upon another to produce its effect. (5) Fifthly, inasmuch as to be able to produce something does not imply any imperfection - a point evident from conclusion eight of chapter two - it follows that this ability can exist in some nature without imperfection. But if every cause depends upon some prior cause, then efficiency would never be found without imperfection. Consequently, an independent power to produce something can exist in some nature and this is simply first. Therefore, such an efficient power is possible and this suffices for now, since we shall prove later from that that it exists in reality. And so A becomes evident from these five arguments.

3.14 Proof of B: If we assume an infinity of accidentally ordered causes, it is clear that these are not concurrent, but one succeeds another so that the second, though it is in some way from the preceding, does not depend upon it for the exercise of its causality. For it is equally effective whether the preceding cause exists or not. A son in turn may beget a child just as well whether his father be dead or alive. But an infinite succession of such causes is impossible unless it exists in virtue of some nature of infinite duration from which the whole succession and every part thereof depends. For no change of form is perpetuated save in virtue of something permanent which is not a part of that succession, since everything of this succession which is in flux is of the same nature. Something essentially prior to the series, then, exists, for everything that is part of the succession depends upon it, and this dependence is of a different order from that by which it depends upon the immediately preceding cause where the latter is a part of the succession. Therefore B is evident.

3.15 Proof of C: From the first conclusion, some nature is able to produce an effect. But if an essential order of agents be denied, then this nature capable of causing does not cause in virtue of some other cause, and even if we assume that in one individual it is caused, nevertheless in some other it will not be caused, and this is what we propose to prove to be true of the first nature. For if we assume that in every individual this nature is caused, then a contradiction follows if we deny the existence of an essential order, since no nature that is caused can be assumed to exist in each individual in such a way that it is included in an accidental order of causes without being at the same time essentially ordered to some other nature. This follows from B.

3.16 (Third conclusion) *If what is able to cause effectively is simply first, then it is itself incapable of being caused, since it cannot be produced and is independently able to produce its effects.*

3.17 This is clear from the second conclusion, for if such a being could cause only in virtue of something else or if it could be produced, then either a process *ad infinitum* or a circle in causes would result, or else the series would terminate in some being which cannot be produced and yet independently is able to produce an effect. This latter being I call "first," and from what you grant, it is clear that anything other than this is not first. Furthermore, it follows that if the first cannot be produced, then it has no causes whatsoever, for it cannot be the result of a final cause (from conclusion two of chapter two) - nor of a material cause (from the sixth conclusion of the same) - nor of a formal cause (from the seventh conclusion there). Neither can it be caused by matter and form together (from the eighth conclusion there).

3.18 (Fourth conclusion) *A being able to exercise efficient causality which is simply first actually exists, and some nature actually existing is capable of exercising such causality.*

3.19 Proof of this: Anything to whose nature it is repugnant to receive existence from something else, exists of itself if it is able to exist at all. To receive existence from something else is repugnant to the very notion of a being which is first in the order of efficiency, as is clear from the third conclusion. And it can exist, as is clear from the second conclusion. Indeed, the fifth argument there which seems to be less conclusive than the others established this much. The other proofs there can be considered in the existential mode - in which case they concern contingent, though manifest facts - or they can be understood of the nature, the quiddity and possibility, in which case the conclusions proceed from necessary premises. From all this it follows that an efficient cause which is first in the unqualified sense of the term can exist of itself, for what does not actually exist of itself is incapable of existing of itself. Otherwise a nonexistent being would cause something to exist; but this is impossible, even apart from the fact that in such a case the thing would be its own cause and hence could not be entirely uncaused.

Another way to establish this fourth conclusion would be to argue from the impropriety of a universe that would lack the highest possible degree of being.

3.20 As a corollary of this fourth conclusion, note that not only is such a cause prior to all others, but that it would be contradictory to say that another is prior to it. And insofar as such a cause is first, it exists. This is proved in the same way as was the fourth conclusion. The very notion of such a being implies its inability to be caused. Therefore, if it can exist, owing to the fact that to be is not contradictory to it, then it follows that it can exist of itself and consequently that it does exist of itself.

3.21 (Fifth conclusion) *A being unable to be caused is of itself necessarily existent.*

3.22 Proof: By excluding every cause of existence other than itself, whether it be intrinsic or extrinsic, we make it impossible for it not to be. Proof: Nothing can be nonexistent unless something either positively or privatively incompatible with it can exist, for one of two contradictories is always true.

Reading Two
Ordinatio I, distinction 44.
God's Absolute and Ordained Powers[2]

In this forty-fourth distinction - where the Master [Peter Lombard] whether God could have made things better than he did - I raise question: Could God have made things otherwise than he has ordered them to be made?

I reply:

In every agent acting intelligently and voluntarily that can act in conformity with an upright or just law but does not have to do so of necessity, one can distinguish between its ordained power and its absolute power. The reason is that either it can act in conformity with some right and just law, and then it is acting according to its ordained power (for it is ordained insofar as it is a principle for doing something in conformity with a right or just law), or else it can act beyond or against such a law, and in this case its absolute power exceeds its ordained power. And therefore it is not only in God, but in every free agent that can either act in accord with the dictates of a just law or go beyond or against that law, that one distinguishes between absolute and ordained power; therefore, the jurists say that someone can act *de facto*, that is, according to his absolute power, or *de jure*, that is, according to his ordained legal power.

But when that upright law - according to which an agent must act in order to act ordinately - is not in the power of that agent, then its absolute power cannot exceed its ordained power in regard to any object without it acting disorderly or inordinately. For, as regards such an agent, the law must remain in force, but an action that is not in conformity with this right and just law will be neither right nor ordinate, because the agent is bound to act in accord with that regulation to which it is subject. Hence all who are subject to a divine law, if they do not act according to it, act inordinately.

But whenever the law and its rectitude are in the power of the agent, so that the law is right only because it has been established, then the agent can freely order things otherwise than this right law dictates and still can act orderly, because he can establish another: right or just law according to which he may act orderly. In such a case it is not simply necessary that his absolute power exceed his ordered power, because his action might still be ordered according to another law just as it had been earlier, but he would still exceed his ordained power according to the prior law if he acted beyond or against such. This could be illustrated in the case of a ruler and his subjects in regard to a positive law.

Applying this to the issue at hand, I say that there are some general laws, ordering things rightly, that have been set up beforehand by the divine will and not by the divine intellect, as something antecedent to any act of the divine will, as was said in dist. 38. But when the intellect presents such a law to the divine will, for instance, "Everyone to be glorified must first be in a state of grace," if it pleases his free will, then it becomes a right or just law, and so too with other laws.

God, therefore, insofar as he is able to act in accord with those right laws he set up previously, is said to act according to his ordained power; but insofar as he is able to do many things that are not in accord with, but go beyond, these preestablished laws, God is said to act according to his absolute power. For God can do anything that is not self-contradictory or act in any way that does not include a contradiction (and there are many such ways he could act); and then he is said to be acting according to his absolute power.

Hence, I say that many other things can be done orderly; and many things that do not include a contradiction other than those that conform to present laws can occur in an ordained way when the rectitude of such law - according to which one acts rightly and orderly - lies in the power of the agent himself. And therefore such an agent can act otherwise, so that he establishes another upright law, which, if it were set up by God, would be right, because no law is right except insofar as the divine will accepts it as established. And in such a case the absolute power of the agent in regard to something would not extend to anything other than what might happen ordinately if it occurred, not indeed ordainedly with respect to this present order, but ordinately with reference to some other order that the divine will could set up if it were able to act in such a way.

Keep in mind also that what is ordained and happens regularly can occur in two ways:

One way is with reference to a universal order. This would involve common law, like the common law that ordains that "every impenitent sinner must be damned" (as if a king were to establish the law that every murderer is to die). The second way is with reference to a particular order. This involves a particular judgment or decision that does not pertain to a universal law, since a law has to do with cases in general, whereas in a singular case what is involved is not a general law, but rather a decision according to law about something that is against the law (for instance, a decision that this murderer is to die).

I say, therefore, that God can act otherwise than is prescribed not only by a particular order, but also by a universal order or law of justice, and in so doing he could still act ordainedly, because what God could do by his absolute power that is either beyond or runs counter to the present order, he could do ordainedly.

But we speak of ordained power in reference only to an order established by a universal law, and not to that which rightly holds by law for a particular case. This is clear from the fact that it is possible for God to save one whom he does not actually save, a living sinner who will die, however, without repenting and will be damned. Admittedly, however, God could not in the same way save Judas, who is already damned. (But for God's absolute power not even this is impossible, since it does not include a contradiction.) It is impossible, therefore, to save Judas in the same way it is possible to save this other sinner, since it is true that the latter could be saved by God's ordained power, whereas Judas could not. And God could save the sinner not just by a particular order (which is concerned, as it were, with only this specific action and particular operation), but by one that is universal, because if he were to save this sinner, he could still do so within the framework of his preestablished just and right laws about the salvation and damnation of individuals. For the salvation of such a sinner is still consistent with the decree "One who remains evil to the end, will be damned" (which is a preestablished law about those who will be damned). The reason is that this sinner has not yet died in sin, and can still cease to be a sinner (especially while still in this life). By his grace God could prevent him from dying impenitent - like a king who prevents someone from killing, and then if he does not condemn the man, he is not violating his universal law against homicide. But it is not consistent with the particular law he did establish that he could save Judas. God could foresee that Judas could be saved by his ordained power - not what is now his ordained power, for at present Judas could only be saved by God's absolute power; but Judas's salvation could have been accomplished by God's ordained power in another order he might have set up.

Reading Three
Haecceitas: Ordinatio II, distinction 3, nn 172, 175; 187-188.
Individuation, Universals, and Common Nature[3]

As was stated in the solution to the first question on this matter [of individuation], nature is prior naturally to "this nature," and the unity proper - which follows on nature *qua* nature - is prior naturally to its unity *qua* this nature. And it is under this prior aspect that there is a metaphysical consideration of the nature, and its definition is assigned and propositions are true in the first mode of *per se* predication. And therefore in the same thing that is one in number, there is some entity to which is attributed a unity that is less than numerical, and that unity is real; and that to which such a unity pertains is made formally "one *de se*" by numerical unity. Therefore, I concede that this real unity is not something existing in two individuals but in one....

And so I concede that whatever is in this stone is one numerically either primarily or *per se* or derivatively. That [individuating difference or haecceity] through which such unity pertains to this composite would perhaps be such primarily; this stone would be such per se, [for] that which is primarily one by this unity [or individuating difference] is a *per se* part of the "this"; that potential [i.e., the stone-nature, in itself less than numerically one] which is perfected by this actual [individuating difference] is only derivatively one numerically with respect to its actuality....

And if you ask me, What is this "individuating entity" from which the individual difference is taken? Is it matter or form or the composite? I give you this answer: Every quidditative entity - be it partial or total - of any sort is of itself indifferent as a quidditative entity to this entity and that, so that as a quidditative entity it is naturally prior to this entity as just this. Now just as, in this natural priority, it does not pertain to it to be this, neither is it repugnant to its essential nature to be other than just *this*. And as the composite does not include *qua* nature its entity whereby it is this matter, nor does its form *qua* nature include its entity whereby it is this form.

This [individuating] entity, therefore, is not the matter or the form or the composite insofar as each of these is a "nature"; rather, it is the ultimate reality of the being that is the matter or that is the form or that is the composite; so that whatever is common and nevertheless determinable, no matter how much it is only one real thing, we can still distinguish further several formally distinct realities, of which this formally is not that; and this is formally the entity of singularity, and that is formally the entity of a nature. Nor can these two realities ever be two distinct real things, in the way that one reality might be that from which the genus is taken and another reality that from which the difference is taken (from which two realities the specific reality as a whole is taken); rather, in the same real thing there are always formally distinct realities (be they in the same real part or the same real whole).

Reading Four
Univocity of Being: *Ordinatio* I, distinction 3,
nn, 25-30; 35-36; 39-40; 56-57.
The Nature of Our Concepts of God[4]

A. We Have Naturally Concepts By Which We Conceive God *Per Se* And Quidditatively.

I say to begin with, therefore, that it is naturally possible to have not only a concept in which God is known incidentally, for example, in some attribute, but also some concept in which he is conceived per se and quidditatively. I prove this, because in conceiving "wise," we conceive a property, according to him [Henry of Ghent], or a quasi-property, which perfects the nature as some further actuality. Hence in order to conceive "wise," it is necessary to think of some quiddity in which this quasi-property exists. And thus it is necessary to look beyond the ideas of all properties or quasi-properties to some quidditative concept to which we attribute these; and this concept will be a quidditative concept of God, because in no other sort will our quest cease.

B. God Is Thought Of In Some Concept Univocal To Himself And Creatures.

Second, I say that God is thought of not only in some concept analogous to that of a creature, that is, one entirely different from what is predicated of a creature, but also in some concept univocal to himself and to a creature. And lest there be any contention about the word "univocation," I call that concept univocal that has sufficient unity in itself that to affirm and deny it of the same subject suffices as a contradiction. It also suffices as a syllogistic middle term, so that where two terms are united in a middle term that is one in this fashion, they are inferred without a fallacy of equivocation to be united among themselves.

And understanding univocation in this sense, I prove it first thus: Every intellect that is certain about one concept and dubious about others has the concept about which it is certain as other than the dubious concepts. The subject [of this proposition] includes the predicate. But the intellect of a person in this life can be certain that God is a being while doubting whether this being is finite or infinite, created or uncreated; therefore the concept of God as a being is other than this or that concept; and although included in each of these, it is none of them of itself, and therefore it is univocal.

Proof of the major [premise]: A certain concept is not the same as a dubious concept, and therefore it is other (which is our proposal), or there is no concept, and then there will be no certitude about any concept.

Proof of the minor: Each philosopher was certain that what he proposed as a first principle was a being; for instance, one as regards fire, another as regards water - each was sure this was a being. But he was not certain that it was a created being or an uncreated one, or whether it was first or not first. He was not certain it was first, for then he would have been certain about something false, and what is false is not scientifically knowable. Nor was he certain it was not first, or he would not have claimed the opposite.

This reason is also confirmed, for someone, seeing that philosophers disagree, could have been certain that what someone had proposed as a first principle was a being, and still, because of the contrariety of their opinions, could be in doubt whether [the first principle] would be this being or that. And if, to such a doubter, a demonstration would either verify or destroy some one alternative - for example, that fire will not be the first being but something posterior to the first being - this would not destroy his first certain notion of it as a being; rather, that notion would survive in the particular conception proved about fire. And this proves the proposition proposed above in the final inference from reason, [namely], that this certain concept, which of itself is neither of the doubtful ones, is preserved in both of them.

Perhaps you do not accept the force of the argument based on the diversity of the opinions of the philosophers, but instead

you say that each thinker has in his intellect two similar concepts that only appear to be one concept because of their analogous resemblance. One can argue against this objection in the
following way. If you accept this evasion, then it appears to destroy every way of proving the unity of some univocal concept.
So, for instance, if you say that "man" is one concept pertaining
to Socrates and Plato, then it will be denied, and one can claim
that there are two concepts that only seem to be one because of
a great resemblance....

My second principal argument runs thus. No real concept is
caused naturally in the intellect in our present state except
through those agents that naturally move our intellect. But the
natural agents are the sense image - or the object revealed in
the sense image - and the active intellect. Therefore, no simple
concept naturally arises in our intellect unless it can come about
by virtue of these causes. Now, the active intellect and the sense
image cannot give rise to a concept that, with respect to the
object revealed in the sense image, is not univocal but rather, in
accordance with an analogical relationship, is altogether other
and higher than the object. It follows that such an "other," analogous concept will never arise in the intellect in our present state.
Also it would thus follow that one could not naturally have any
concept of God - which is false.

The assumption is proved thus. At the limit of its causal power,
any object, whether revealed in the sense image or in the intelligible species, cooperates with the causality of the passive or
active intellect and brings about as its adequate effect either its
own proper concept or a concept of all that is essentially or virtually included in it. But this "other" concept which is thought
to be analogous is not included in the causal object either essentially or virtually - nor is it a proper concept of the object. Therefore, this analogous concept cannot be produced by such an efficient agent [namely, by the object revealed in the image or spe-
cies].

This argument based on the role of the object is confirmed in
the following way. With the exception of its own proper adequate
concept and whatever is included in it in either of the afore-

mentioned ways, the object can only be the source of knowing something else through discursive reasoning. But discursive reasoning presupposes a prior grasp of the simple things toward which one reasons. Based on this, a proof can be formulated thus. No object produces both a simple proper concept [of itself] and in the same intellect the simple proper concept of another object, unless the former object contains the latter essentially or virtually. However, no created object essentially or virtually contains an uncreated object, at least not under the formality by which what is essentially posterior is related to what is essentially prior. Indeed, it is contrary to the very idea of being essentially posterior that it virtually include what is prior to it. And with respect to something that is altogether proper to the uncreated and not just common to it, it is evident that a created object does not essentially contain the uncreated. Therefore, it does not produce a simple concept that is proper to the uncreated being.

[It is also argued in this way:] The manner in which every metaphysical inquiry about God proceeds is by considering the formal notion of something and taking away from that formal notion the imperfection that it has in creatures while retaining that formal meaning and completely attributing to it the highest perfection, and thus ascribing it to God. For example, take the formal notion of wisdom (or of the intellect) or of the will: it may be considered in itself and without qualification; and from the fact that this notion implies no imperfection or limitation, the imperfections that accompany it in creatures are removed from it; and, keeping the same meaning of wisdom and of will, these are attributed to God in a most perfect way. Therefore, every inquiry about God presupposes that the intellect has the same univocal concept that it received from creatures.

And if you say that the formal notion is other as regards those things that pertain to God, a disconcerting consequence results, [namely], that from the proper notion of anything found in creatures nothing can be inferred about God, because the notion of what each has is entirely different; indeed, there is no more reason to conclude that God is formally wise from the notion of wisdom that we perceive in creatures than [there is to conclude] that God is formally a stone; for some concept other than the concept of a created stone can be formed that bears a relationship to the concept of a stone as an idea in God, and therefore one can say, "God is formally a stone," according to this analogous conception, just as he can be said to be "wise" according to that [other] analogous concept....

C. God Is Not Known Naturally In The Present Life In A Particular, Proper Way.

Thirdly, I say that God is not known naturally by one in the present life in a particular and proper way, that is, under the aspect of his [unique] essence as it is in itself and as it is just this. But the reason given for this in the preceding opinion [of Henry of Ghent] is not conclusive....

Hence, there is another reason for this conclusion, namely, that God as "this essence" in itself is not known naturally by us, because under this aspect such a knowable thing is a voluntary object. Only for the divine intellect would it be a natural object. And therefore by no created intellect can it be naturally known under the aspect of this essence insofar as it is just this. Neither is there some essence naturally knowable to us that reveals this [unique] essence as just this, whether by reason of a likeness of univocation or of imitation. For only in general notions is there univocation; imitation also is deficient, because it is imperfect, since creatures imperfectly imitate him....

Reading Five
Quodlibet 6, 6.17-6.20.
Abstraction and Intuition[5]

6.17 [Second proof from reason] A second argument from reason is this: The mode characteristic of the beatific object *qua* beatific object exists in reality and extramentally. But intensive infinity is this kind of mode in the divine essence. Therefore, it exists there extramentally and consequently magnitude does also.

6.18 [Proof of the major based on the distinction between intuitive and abstract cognition] Proof of the major is found in the perfection of the beatific act. To understand better what is involved, it is helpful to distinguish two acts of the intellect at the level of simple apprehension or intellection of a simple object. One is indifferent as to whether the object is existing or not, and also whether it is present in reality or not. We often experience this act in ourselves, for universals and the essences of things we grasp equally well whether they exist extramentally in some subject or not or whether we have an instance of them actually present or not. We also have [an empirical or] a *posteriori* proof of this, for scientific knowledge of a conclusion or understanding of a principle can be equally present to the intellect whether what they are about is existing or not, or is present or absent. In either case, then, one can have an equal understanding of that term on which an understanding of the principle or conclusion depends. This act of understanding, which can be called "scientific," because it is a prerequisite condition for knowing the conclusion and understanding the principle, can very appropriately be called "abstractive" because it "abstracts" the object from existence or non-existence, from presence or absence.

But there is another act of understanding, though we do not experience it in ourselves as certainly, but it is possible. It is knowledge precisely of a present object as present and of an existing object as existing. Proof of this: Every perfection which is a perfection of cognition absolutely and which can be present in a faculty of sense knowledge can pertain eminently to an intellective cognitional faculty. But it is a matter of perfection in the act of knowing *qua* knowledge that what is first known be attained perfectly, and this is so when it is attained in itself and not just in some diminished or derivative likeness of itself. On the other hand, a sense power has such perfection in its knowledge, because it can attain an object in itself as existing and present in its real existence, and not just diminutively in a kind of imperfect likeness of itself. Therefore this perfection also pertains to an intellective power in the act of knowing. It could not pertain to it however unless it could know an existing thing and know it as present either in its own existence or in some intelligible object that contains the thing in question in an eminent way, which we are not concerned with at present.

Such knowledge of the existent *qua* existent and present is something an angel has about himself. For Michael does not know himself in the way he would know Gabriel if Gabriel were annihilated, viz., by abstractive cognition, but he knows himself as existing and as existing in a way that is identical with himself. He also is aware of his intellection in this way if he reflects upon it, considering it not just as any object in which one has abstracted from existence or non-existence in the way he would think of another angel's knowledge, if such did not actually exist; rather he knows himself to be knowing, that is to say, he knows his knowledge as something existing in himself. This knowledge possible for an angel, therefore, is also simply possible for our intellective power, because we have the promise that we shall be like the angels. Now this sort of intellection can properly be called "intuitive," because it is an intuition of a thing as existing and present.

Applying this to the case at hand, we can say that the beatific act of the intellect cannot be one of abstractive cognition; it must be intuitive. Since abstractive cognition concerns equally the existent and the nonexistent, if the beatific act were of this sort one could be beatifically happy with a nonexistent object, which is impossible. Also, abstractive knowledge is possible where the object is not attained in itself but only in some likeness. Beatitude, on the contrary, can never be found unless the beatific object is reached immediately and in itself. And this intuitive intellection is what some call, and rightly so, face-to-face vision, basing themselves on the words of the Apostle: "We see now through a mirror in an obscure manner, but then face to face." (1 Cor. 13:12)

From this the major is manifest. If the beatific act is necessarily an intuition of its object, then it is knowledge of that object as existing and as present in its own existence. Therefore, every condition that is required *per se* of a beatific object must pertain to it *per se* in its real existence, and indeed in its real existence as something present. Hence we have our major.

Notes

[1]Allan B. Wolter, *John Duns Scotus: A Treatise on God as First Principle* (Chicago: Franciscan Herald Press, 1966), 42-54.

[2]Allan B. Wolter, *Duns Sotus on the Will and Morality* (Washington, D.C.: Catholic University of America Press, 1986) 255-261; 1997 English only version (191-194). Reprinted with permission.

[3]William M. Frank, *Duns Scotus, Metaphysician* (West Lafayette, Indiana: Purdue University Press, 1995), 185-187. Reprinted with permission.

[4]William A. Frank, *Duns Scotus, Metaphysician* (West Lafayette, Indiana: Purdue University Press, 1995), 109-117. Reprinted with permission.

[5]John Duns Scotus, *God and Creatures: The Quodlibetal Questions*, translated with an introduction, notes and glossary by Felix Allunis and Allan B. Wolter (Princeton, NJ: Princeton University Press, 1975), 135-137. Reprinted with permission.

Appendix Two

Reading One
Ordinatio III, distinction 7, question 3.
The Predestination of Christ and His Mother[1]

I ask: Was Christ predestined to be the Son of God? ...

I reply: Predestination consists in foreordaining someone first of all to glory and then to other things which are ordered to glory. Now the human nature in Christ was predestined to be glorified, and in order to be glorified, it was predestined to be united to the Word, in as much as such glory as it was granted would never have been conferred on this nature had it not been so united. Now if it would not be fitting to ordain one to such glory if certain merits were absent, whereas it would be fitting if they were present, then such merits are included in the predestination. And so it would seem that this union by way of fitness is ordered to this glory, although it is not exactly as merit that it falls under this predestination. And just as it is foreordained that this nature be united to the Word, so it is predestined that the Word be man and that this man be the Word.

But you may object that primarily predestination regards the person and hence one must first find some person to whom God predestined (1) the glory and then (2) this union with reference to the glory. Now you will find no divine Person to whom God predestined this union [as a means of glory]. Obviously he did not do so to the Word in so far as he is the Word. Neither was this union predestined as a means of glory to the Word as subsisting in a human nature, because to the extent that he subsists in this way, the union is already included.

I reply: we can deny that predestination concerns persons only, for if God can love a good other than himself, not only when it is a person, but also when it is a nature, then for its sake he can also select and ordain in advance some good suitable to it. Consequently, he can choose (1) glory and (2) the union as a means of glory, not only for the person, but also for some nature. It is true, however, that in all cases other than this, predestination does concern the person, for in no other instance has God foreordained a good to a [human] nature without by that very fact foreordaining it also to some person, for the simple reason that no other human nature subsists save in a created person to whom the good can be foreordained. But in our case this is not so.

At this point, however, two doubts arise. First, does this predestination depend necessarily upon the fall of human nature? Many authorities seem to say as much when they declare the Son of God would never have become incarnate had man not fallen.

Without passing judgment it can be said that so far as priority of objects intended by God is concerned, the predestination of anyone to glory is prior by nature to the prevision of the sin or damnation of anyone (according to the final opinion given in distinction forty-one of the first book). So much the more then is this true of the predestination of (that soul) which was destined beforehand to possess the very highest glory possible. For it seems to be universally true that one who wills ordinately, and not inordinately, first intends what is nearer the end, and just as he first intends one to have glory before grace, so among those to whom he has foreordained glory, he who wills ordinately, would seem to intend first the glory of the one he wishes to be nearest the end, and therefore he intends glory to this soul [of Christ] before he wills glory to any other soul, and to every other soul he wills glory before taking into account the opposite of these habits [namely, the sin or damnation of anyone].

Authorities to the contrary can all be explained in the sense that Christ would not have come as redeemer, if man had not sinned. Perhaps, too, he would not have been able to suffer, since there would have been no need of a union with a passible body for this soul glorified from its first moment of existence, to which God chose to give not only the highest glory but also willed that it be always present. If man had not sinned, of course, there would have been no need of a redemption. Still it does not seem to be solely because of the redemption that God predestined this soul to such glory, since the redemption or the glory of the souls to be redeemed is not comparable to the glory of the soul of Christ. Neither is it likely that the highest good in the whole of creation is something that merely chanced to take place. And that only because of some lesser good. Nor is it probable that God predestined Adam to such a good before he predestined Christ. Yet all this would follow, yes, and even something more absurd. If the predestination of Christ's soul was for the sole purpose of redeeming others, it would follow that in foreordaining Adam to glory God would have had to foresee him as having fallen into sin before he could have predestined Christ to glory.

Consequently, we can say that God selected for his heavenly choir all the angels and men he wished to have with their varied degrees of perfection, and all this before considering either the sin or the punishment of the sinner. No one therefore is predestined simply because God foresaw another would fall, lest anyone have reason to rejoice at the misfortune of another.

Our second doubt is this: Which did God intend first, the union of this nature with the Word, or its ordination to glory? Now the sequence in which the creative artist evolves his plan is the very opposite of the way he puts it into execution. One can say, however, that in the order of execution God's union with a human nature is naturally prior to his granting it the greatest grace and glory. We could presume, then, that it was in the reverse order that he intended them, so that God would first intend that some nature, not the highest, should receive the highest glory, proving thereby he was not constrained to grant glory in the same measure as he bestowed natural perfection. Then secondly, as it were, he willed that this nature should subsist in the Person of the Word, so that the angel might not be subject to a [mere] man.

Reading Two
Ordinatio III, distinction 3, question 1.
The Immaculate Conception of the Blessed Virgin[2]

To the question I say that God could have brought it about that [1] she was never in original sin, or [2] she was in sin for only an instant, or [3] she was in sin for some period of time and at the last instant of that time was purged of it.

[Re 1] I declare the first to be possible, because grace is equivalent to original justice so far as divine acceptance goes, so that because of this grace there is no original sin in the soul that possesses it. God could have at the very first instant infused into this soul grace to such a degree as was given to other souls at the time of circumcision or of baptism; therefore in the first instant the soul would not have original sin, just as a baptized person would also not have it afterwards. And if the infection of the flesh was there in the first instant, it was not the necessary cause of the infection of the soul, just as neither after baptism when - according to many - the infection of the flesh remains whereas that of the soul does not; or God could have cleansed the flesh before infusing the soul, so that in that instant it was not infected.

[Re 2] The second possibility is evident, because a natural agent could begin to act in an instant, so that in that instant [just before it begins to act] it would be in a state of rest under one contrary and for the time spent in acting it would be under a contrary form in a state of becoming or flux; but God can act whenever a natural agent can act: therefore at some instant he could cause grace to exist for a stretch of time.

This is confirmed also because, if the soul is in sin for some interval of time, by divine grace it could rather have been in a state of grace during that interval; but from the time when it was conceived it could be in sin [and according to you it was]; therefore it could likewise be in grace, and if it were, it was not necessary that it was in grace at the first instant of that time just it was not necessary concerning mutation and motion.

Furthermore, if in the first instant [God] had created grace, then one could posit the third alternative, and he could have failed to conserve it during the time that ensued.

[Re 3] The third possibility is manifest.

[Scotus' personal position] But which of these three possibilities is factually the case, God knows - but if the authority of the Church or the authority of Scripture does not contradict such, *it seems probable that what is more excellent should be attributed to Mary.*

[Objections re 2] Against the second of these alternatives there is a twofold objection:

First in this way: every action God does with respect to a creature he does in an instant, for - according to Physics VIII - infinite power acts in an instant. Since, a finite and an infinite power cannot act in equal measure; therefore, [God] cannot after an instant of guilt, justify a soul during the stretch of time that follows.

Furthermore, that justification would be either a motion or a mutation. Now it is not a mutation since it would not occur in an instant. Neither is it a movement, for as a succession of movable parts, this would involve something mobile. Now this cannot be: [1] the soul, for that is indivisible; [2] or a form in the soul, namely, grace; [3] or something midway between these extremes, because between privative opposites, namely what the soul is suited by nature - to receive on the one hand and its privation on the other, there is nothing in between, any more than there is between absolute contradictories; [4] or parts acquired or lost in either one of these [i.e., the soul or its grace], since as a subject neither is divisible.

[Answer to the objections] To the first objection, I say that if God acted voluntarily at some instant during some span of time, he would not have to wait for an interval of time before he could act at some determinate instant, but he could act in time without having acted at the first instant of that time-period. Hence, it is true that God could act in an instant as regards anything he did immediately, but it is not necessary that he act instantaneously.

To the second, I say that strictly speaking - in the sense the Philosopher uses the terms "motion" and "mutation" - this passive-justification is neither a movement nor a mutation, but it is something having characteristics of both. - It resembles a mutation inasmuch as it exists as a simple indivisible form in its subject, and it shares with time and movement the fact that it does not exist in some indivisible measure of duration but, unlike a mutation, it takes place in time; but it also is unlike a motion, which is a process or state of flux involving parts of a mobile form; neither are there any intermediate stages between two extremes, because there is nothing in between as the objection proved.

Consider this example: the mobile passes from the form under which it existed at the last moment it was at rest, so that once that instant is past, there is a continuous loss of that form according to its parts and a continuous acquisition of the opposite form. But if during that whole time it was under that opposite form, since it was not successively acquiring parts of it, it would resemble what we are proposing. For then the acquisition of that form will be neither a motion nor a mutation, just as now the transition from an unchanged rest-state to one of motion is in itself neither a mutation nor motion.

But why is the reception of the action of a natural agent either a mutation or a motion, and not this? I reply: if a natural agent can induce a form suddenly, it does so as a mutation, and if it cannot do it suddenly, it is necessary that it act in time, and thus through motion, and so it induces its form by moving [i.e., by changing the patient only gradually]. But God, although he could induce the form in an instant, nevertheless, if he would not induce it for only an instant, he could for a span of time induce the form as a whole and not just one part before the other; for to be able to act in time is not an imperfection in an agent, although it is an imperfection if the agent of necessity has to act in time.

[To the Arguments to the Contrary]

[To the authorities]

But if one holds the answer to the question is negative, the reply to give to all the authorities to the contrary is that every child of Adam begotten in a natural way is a debtor to original justice and lacks it because of Adam's demerit. Therefore every such descendent begotten in a natural way has a basis for contracting original sin. But if someone in the first instance of creation of the soul were given grace, that person would never lack original justice, - and nevertheless this is not something the person has of itself, but merit of another, if it was because of another's merit that grace was conferred on this person.

Therefore, everyone on their own would have original sin unless another prevented it by way of mediation. And in this way the authorities are explained because "all who are the natural progeny of Adam are sinners," i.e., from the manner in which they get their nature from Adam they have no reason to possess the justice they should have had, unless it is given to them in another way. But just as grace could be conferred afterwards, so it could be given at the first instant [the soul was created].

This same explanation answers the arguments given for the first opinion, because Mary most of all needed Christ as a redeemer; for she would have contracted original in by reason of her common birthright were she not prevented by the grace of her mediator, - and just as others would have had a need for Christ that through his merits the sin they had already contracted be remitted, so she had an even greater need of a mediator lest she would need to contract it at somctimc and to prevent her from contracting it....

To the other [second reason] about the opening of the door - it is evident that the door was open to her through the merits of Christ that were foreseen and accepted in a special way for this person, so that because of his passion this person was never in a state of sin and hence there was no reason why the door was closed, although, by reason of her origin, it would have been closed to her just as it was to others.

Reading Three
Ordinatio III, distinction 37
Moral Relationships[3]

To the question, then, I say that some things can be said to belong to the law of nature in two ways:

[1] One way is as first practical principles known from their terms or as conclusions necessarily entailed by them. These are said to belong to the natural law in the strictest sense, and there can be no dispensation in their regard, as the argument for the first opinion proves. It is to these that the canon of the *Decrees of Gratian* refers, where it is said that "the natural law begins from the very beginnings of rational creatures, nor does time change it, but it is immutably permanent" - and this I concede.

But this is not the case when we speak in general of all the precepts of the second table [of the decalogue]. For the reasons behind the commands and prohibitions there are not practical principles that are necessary in an unqualified sense, nor are they simply necessary conclusions from such. For they contain no goodness such as is necessarily prescribed for attaining the goodness of the ultimate end, nor in what is forbidden is there such malice as would turn one away necessarily from the last end, for even if the good found in these maxims were not commanded, the last end [of man as union with God] could still be loved and attained, whereas if the evil proscribed by them were not forbidden, it would still be consistent with the acquisition of the ultimate end.

But it is different with the precepts of the first table, because these regard God immediately as object. Indeed the first two, if they be understood in a purely negative sense - i.e., "You shall not have other gods before me" and "You shall not take the name of the Lord, your God, in vain," i.e., "You should show no irreverence to God" - belong to the natural law, taking law of nature strictly, for this follows necessarily: "If God exists, then he alone must be loved as God." It likewise follows that nothing else must be worshiped as God, nor must any irreverence be shown to him. Consequently, God could not dispense in regard to these so that someone could do the opposite of what this or that prohibits.

The third commandment of the first table is that which concerns the observance of the Sabbath. It is affirmative insofar as it prescribes that some worship be given to God at a specific time, but so far as the specification to this or that time goes, it does not pertain to the law of nature strictly speaking. Similarly with the negative portion included therein, which forbids servile work for a definite time that would interfere with the worship to be shown to him. For such work is only prohibited because it impedes or keeps one from the cult that is commanded.

But there is some doubt whether this precept of observing the Sabbath pertains to the natural law strictly to the extent that it requires that at some definite time worship be shown to God. For if it does not, then God could dispense from it absolutely, so that a man for the entire duration of his life would never have to manifest any affection or love for God. This does not seem probable, for without some act of goodwill or love towards God as the ultimate end, one could not do anything simply good that would be needed to attain that end, and thus this person would never be bound to will anything that is simply good in an unqualified sense. For the same reason that excludes from strict natural law the need to show worship to God now, holds also for then [i.e., the Sabbath] and, by the same token, for any specific time. Therefore, strictly speaking, it is not clear how one could infer that a person is bound then or now to worship God and, by the same reasoning, how anyone is bound at some undefined time to do so, for no one is obliged to perform at some undefined time an act which he is not obligated to perform at some definite time when some opportunities for doing so present themselves.

But if this is strictly of the natural law, so that "God must be loved" follows necessarily from "God must not be hated" or some other such precept, then this argument from singular instances to a universal statement does not hold, but represents a fallacy of a figure of speech, even as does the converse, where one argues from several determinate instances to one indeterminate one. But if this third commandment is not strictly a matter of natural law, then it must be judged like the precepts of the second table of the decalogue.

[2] The other way in which things belong to the law of nature is because they are exceedingly in harmony with that law, even though they do not follow necessarily from those first practical principles known from their terms, principles which are necessarily grasped by any intellect understanding those terms. Now, it is certain that all the precepts of the second table also belong to the natural law in this way, since their rightness is very much in harmony with the first practical principles that are known of necessity.

This distinction can be made clear by an example. Given the principle of positive law that life in a community or state ought to be peaceful, it does not follow from this necessarily that everyone ought to have possessions distinct from those of another, for peace could reign in a group or among those living together, even if everything was common property. Not even in the case of the infirm is private possession an absolute necessity; nevertheless, that such persons have their own possessions is exceedingly consonant with peaceful living, for the infirm care more about goods of their own than they do about common property, and would prefer rather that the common goods be assigned to them than that they be given to the community and its custodian for the common good, and so strife and disorder could occur. And it is this way, perhaps, with all positive laws, for although there is some one principle which serves as the basis for establishing these laws, still positive laws do not follow with simple [logical] necessity from the principle in question or explicate it as regards certain particular cases. Nevertheless, these explications are greatly in harmony with the first universal principle they clarify.

To put all we have said together, first we deny that all the commandments of the second table pertain strictly to the law of nature second, we admit that the first two commandments belong strictly to the law of nature; third, there is some doubt about the third commandment of the first table; fourth, we concede that all the commandments fall under the law of nature, speaking broadly....

And then one could say ... that God has now explained [in the Scriptures] a higher love of neighbor that transcends that which is included in, or follows from, the principles of the law of nature. In other words, although the love of neighbor that can be inferred from principles of the law of nature only requires that we love him in himself, still the love of neighbor as explained [by Christ and Paul] includes willing him these other goods, or at least not wishing him the opposite evils, such as not wanting him to be deprived unjustly of corporeal life, or conjugal fidelity, or temporal goods, and the like. Hence it is true that love of neighbor fulfills the law, viz., in the way it has been explained that this law of love must be observed, although not in the way that love of neighbor follows from the first principles of natural law. In a similar fashion, the whole law so far as the second table and the prophets are concerned - depends on this commandment: "Love your neighbor as yourself," again understanding this not as something that follows of necessity from the first practical principles of the law of nature, but as the Lawgiver intended the love of neighbor to be observed according to the precepts of the second table.

Reading Four
Ordinatio II, distinction 6.
Moral Affections[4]

Justice can be understood to be either infused (which is called
gratuitous or grace), or acquired (which is called moral), or innate (which is the will's liberty itself). For if one were to think,
according to that fictitious situation Anselm postulates in *The
Fall of the Devil*, that there was an angel with an affection for
the beneficial, but without an affection for justice (i.e., one that
had a purely intellectual appetite as such and not one that was
free), such an angel would be unable not to will what is beneficial, and unable not to covet such above all. But this would not
be imputed to it as sin, because this appetite would be related
to intellect as the visual appetite is now related to sight, necessarily following what is shown to it by that cognitive power, and
being inclined to seek the very best revealed by such a power,
for it would have nothing to restrain it. Therefore, this affection
for justice, which is the first checkrein on the affection for the
beneficial, inasmuch as we need not actually seek that towards
which the latter affection inclines us, nor must we seek it above
all else (namely, to the extent to which we are inclined by this
affection for the advantageous) – this affection for what is just,
I say, is the liberty innate to the will, since it represents the
first checkrein on this affection for the advantageous.

Anselm may often be speaking not just of the actual justice
which is acquired, but of infused justice, because he says it is
lost through mortal sin, something true only of infused justice.
Nevertheless by distinguishing from the nature of the thing the
two primary characteristics of this twofold affection (one inclining the will above all to the advantageous, the other moderating it, as it were, lest the will in eliciting an act should have to
follow its inclination), he makes these aspects out to be nothing
other than the will itself insofar as it is an intellective appetite
and insofar as it is free. For, as has been said, *qua* pure intellective appetite, the will would be actually inclined to the opti-
mum intelligible (as sight is to what is best visible), whereas
qua free, it could restrain itself in eliciting its act from following

this natural inclination, as to either the substance of the act or its intensity.

But if some power were exclusively appetitive, following its inclination in acting as the visual appetite follows the visual inclination of the eye (though I admit it could only want what is intelligible, as the visual appetite can only seek what is visible), that power still could not sin in seeking such, for it would be powerless to seek anything other than what the intellect would show it or in any way other than the cognition would incline it. But this same power, having been made free (because we have nothing more here than one thing which includes virtually several perfectional aspects, which it would not include if it lacked that of liberty) – this power, I say, through its liberty could moderate itself in willing. It could do so as regards that volition towards which it is inclined by the affection for the advantageous, even though it might be most inclined to will the advantageous. And from the fact that it could moderate this, it is bound to do so according to the rule of justice it has received from a higher will. It is clear, then, from this that a free will is not bound in every way to seek happiness (in the way a will that was only an intellective appetite without liberty would seek it). Rather it is bound, in eliciting its act, to moderate the appetite qua intellective, which means to moderate the affection for the advantageous, namely, lest it will immoderately.

There are three ways, however, in which a will, able to moderate itself as regards the happiness befitting it, could fail to do so. As to intensity, it might love it more passionately than it deserves. Or through precipitance, it might want it sooner than is becoming. Or with disregard to the proper causal way to obtain it – for instance, it might want it without meriting it – or perhaps for other reasons, all of which one need not bother with here.

Probably in one of these ways, then, the will of the angel went to excess: Either by wanting happiness as a good for him rather than loving it as a good in itself – that is, wanting a good, like the beatific object, to belong exclusively to himself, rather than to be in another such as in his God. And this would be the supreme perversity of the will, which – according to Augustine (*Eighty-three Different Questions*, q. 30 – is to use as means what is to be enjoyed as an end, and treat as an end what is to be used as a means. Or the angel could have failed in the second way, wanting at once what God wished him to have after period of probation. Or it might have been in the third way, by wanting to possess happiness by natural means rather than by earning it by grace, since God wished him to merit it.

His free will, then, should have moderated his desire in such way as right reason had revealed to him. For happiness should have been wanted less for his sake than for the sake of God, and he should have wanted it at the time God intended and on the basis of merit, as planned. If in some such fashion, then, he yielded to this affection for the advantageous, not moderating it through justice, be it infused (if the angel had such), or acquired, or innate (which is liberty itself), then he sinned.

Reading Five
Questions on Metaphysics, IX, question 15.
Rational Freedom[5]

Is the difference that Aristotle assigns between the rational and irrational potencies appropriate, namely, that the former are capable of contrary effects but the latter produce but one effect? ...

Aristotle seems to have understood the distinction to stem from the fact that a natural form is a principle for making only one pair of opposites, that which resembles itself naturally, just as this is this and not its opposite. But a form that is in the intellect, in the way that knowledge informs the mind, is a principle for representing opposites by an intentional likeness, just as knowledge is a virtual likeness of opposites [e.g., medical science is knowledge of both health and sickness], since one of the contraries includes the privation of the other. But the agent is active in regard to what can be modeled according to the form by which it acts. For this reason, then, Aristotle appears to have introduced the distinction....

[K]eep in mind that the primary distinction of active potencies stems from the radically different way in which they elicit their respective operations [rather than from what they are concerned with]. For if we can somehow distinguish them because one acts in regard to this, another in regard to that, such a distinction is not so immediate [i.e., radical or basic]. For a power or potency is related to the object in regard to which it acts only by means of some operation that it elicits in one way or another, and there is only a twofold generic way that an operation proper to a potency can be elicited. For either the potency of itself is determined to act, so that so far as it is concerned, it cannot fail to act when not impeded from without; or it is not of itself so determined but can perform either this act or its opposite or can either act or not act at all. A potency of the first sort is commonly called nature, whereas one of the second sort is called will. Hence, the primary division of active potencies is into nature and will – a distinction that Aristotle had in mind in book

2 of *Physics* when he assumed that there were two incidental, or *per accidens*, efficient causes: chance, which is reducible to nature; and fortune, which involves purpose or will.

Suppose someone seeks a further reason for this distinction. Just why does nature have to do with only one sort of action? That is, if it has to do with this or that, why is it determined of itself to cause just this effect or these effects, whatever they may be, whereas will, by contrast, has alternatives, that is, it is not intrinsically determined to this action or its opposite, or for that matter to acting or not acting at all? One could reply to such a question that there is no further reason for this. Just as any immediate effect is related to its immediate cause primarily and per se, without benefit of any mediating cause – otherwise one could go on ad infinitum looking for reasons – so an active cause [as opposed to a material or other cause] seems to be immediately related to the action that it elicits. One can give no other reason why it elicits its action in this way except that it is this sort of cause. Yet this is precisely what one is [foolishly] asking a reason for. "Heat heats" because it is heat, and the proposition "Heat heats" is not a mediate proposition [i.e., it is not a conclusion] but is rather a primary proposition in the fourth mode of per se predication, as is also the proposition "Heat is determined of itself to heat." "The will wills" and "The will does not will in a definite way by reason of some intrinsically necessary specification" would be similar sorts of statements.

[*Two objections*] Against this it is first objected that the proposition "The will wills" is contingent. If the will were not determined of itself to will, how would any contingent proposition be immediate?

Second, there is this objection. Why postulate this indeterminacy in the will if it cannot be proved to follow from the nature of the will? [In which case "The will wills" would be a conclusion and not a per se proposition of the fourth mode.]

[Solutions] The answer to the first is that the contingent does not follow from the necessary. This is clear if you consider some contingent proposition. If it is immediate, we have what we seek;

if not, then there is some proposition that is intermediate; but this other premise from which it follows is also contingent; otherwise, a contingent proposition could be inferred from necessary premises [which is logically impossible]. But if this intermediate premise is contingent [according to the objector], there must be some further contingent proposition from which it follows; and so ad infinitum, unless one stops with some proposition that is admittedly immediate [or axiomatic].

What Aristotle says near the end of the *Posterior Analytics*, book 1, confirms this. There his meaning is that opining occurs both as a truth that is "propter quid" (that is, it is expressed in terms of a first principle or immediate proposition) and as a factual, or "quia," proposition that needs further proof. And so it is with the proposition under consideration, "The will wills A." If there is no further cause or mediate reason why this is the case, then our proposal is conceded [namely, that it is a first, or per se, proposition]. If there is some reason or cause, such as "Because the will wills B," then one inquires further. Somewhere, however, you must stop. Where? Why does the will will this last? There is no other cause to be found except that the will is will. And yet if this last proposition were necessary, it could not be the sole premise from which something contingent followed.

As for the second objection [i.e., that indeterminacy must be proved from the nature of the will and hence a priori], the proof here is a posteriori, for the person who wills [some object] experiences that he could have nilled or not willed what he did, according to what has been explained more at length elsewhere about the will's liberty.

[*A doubt*] A further doubt arises about the aforesaid. What reduces such a potency to act if it is of itself undetermined toward acting or not acting?

I reply: there is a certain indeterminacy of insufficiency, based on potentiality and a defect of actuality, in the way, for instance, that matter without a form is indeterminate as regards the actuation given by the form. There is another indeterminacy, however, that of a superabundant sufficiency, based on unlimited actuality, either in an unqualified or in a qualified sense.

The first sort of indeterminacy is not reduced to actuality unless it first is determined to some form by something else. Something indeterminate in the second sense, however, can determine itself. If this could occur where some limited actuality exists, how much more where the actuality is unlimited! For it would lack nothing required for an acting principle. Otherwise, God – who, in virtue of his indeterminacy of unlimited actuality, is supremely underdetermined in regard to any action whatsoever – would be unable to do anything of himself, which is false. Take this example: fire has the ability to heat, neither do we seek anything extrinsic to fire itself that determined it to burn. Suppose, without losing any of its perfection as heat, it were given the perfection of coldness, why should it not be able to determine itself to heat something, as before?... But the indetermination ascribed to the will is not like that of matter, nor, insofar as it is active, is it the indeterminacy of imperfection; rather it is the indeterminacy of surpassing perfection and power, not restricted to some specific act....

[*Reply to an initial argument*] [I]t is clear that a rational potency, such as the will is said to be, does not have to perform opposites simultaneously but rather can determine itself to either alternative, which is something that the intellect cannot do. When it is objected that I am unable to be not seated, on the assumption I am sitting, my answer is this: A proposition about the possible would be false in the composite sense, because it would imply that I could do both at once. In the divided sense, however, some would say that when the sitting occurs, this is so necessarily, according to that principle in *De interpretatione*, "That which is must needs be when it is," and that nothing else is possible then but only at the moment before, when the present situation could have been otherwise. And these persons see no way of saving the claim that *now* the will has a potency for the opposite of the state it is actually in. This is absurd, however, for it would mean that necessity and contingency are not properly conditions of being at the time they exist. But if that were true, necessity and contingency would never exist, for when something is not existent, it is neither necessary nor contingent. It would take too long, however, to explain now why the *De interpretatione* principle does not support their claims, because their argument is invalid on three counts, being an instance of the fallacy of consequent, of figure of speech, and of the simple and qualified sense. To put the matter in another way, one could say that when the will is in a certain state of volition, it is in that state contingently, and that its present volition stems from it contingently, for if it does not do so then, it will never do so, since at no other time does it proceed from the will.

And just as this particular volition is contingently in the will, at that very moment the will is a potency with power over its opposite; and this holds for that moment in the divided sense not that it could will the opposite at the same time as it wills this, but in the sense that it has the power to will the contrary at that very instant by not willing the other at that instant. For at this very instant it could, nevertheless, posit the other, in a divided sense, and do this not necessarily but contingently.

Notes

[1]John Duns Scotus: *Four Questions on Mary*, translated with an introduction and notes by Allan B. Wolter (St. Bonaventure, NY: The Franciscan Institute, 2000), 21-27.

[2]John Duns Scotus: *Four Questions on Mary*, translated with an introduction and notes by Allan B. Wolter (St. Bonaventure, NY: The Franciscan Institute, 2000), 43-53.

[3]Allan B. Wolter, *Duns Sotus on the Will and Morality*, 1997 ed. (Washington, D.C.: Catholic University of America Press, 1986) 202-206. Reprinted with permission.

[4]Allan B. Wolter, *Duns Sotus on the Will and Morality* (Washington, D.C.: Catholic University of America Press, 1986) 469-473; 1997 edition: 298-300. Reprinted with permission.

[5]William M. Frank, *Duns Scotus, Metaphysician* (West Lafayette, Indiana: Purdue University Press, 1995), 187-195. Reprinted with permission.

Appendix Three

Reading One
Quodlibet 4, article 3, 4.61-4.63.
Divine Persons in the Trinity[1]

From What Considerations could One Prescind and still have the First Person?

4.61 Given the two conclusions [of 4.48], viz., that the first person's relationship of origin to the second is only one thing in reality but is conceptually distinguished, we can make clear to what extent the first person is separable apart from this relationship of origin to the second. If this means separable in reality, this is clearly false. Neither is there any need to distinguish this or that aspect of the relationship, for in reality it is but one single thing. If this were really removed, what is constituted by it would not remain either. If one means separable conceptually without contradiction, however, in the sense that the notion of the first person in the mind is separable from the notion of the relationship of origin between the first and second person, we must, it seems, make use of the distinction cited between the diverse ways of considering that one relationship. Of course if one abstracts or prescinds from all the ways at once, the mind will have no conception whatsoever of a suppositum related by such a relationship of origin. It is contradictory that an intellect should conceive the complete absence of any relationship of origin in a suppositum and still conceive of a suppositum related by such a relationship. There is no contradiction, however, that the suppositum considered according to a prior reason should be conceivable apart from the relationship considered under some posterior reason or aspect. Now these diverse aspects in our mind would have that order of prior or posterior conceivability they would be apt to have in those objects suited to move our intellect.

4.62 Now perhaps one could without contradiction think of someone subsisting incommunicably apart from a relationship of origin to the second person if he were viewed under some special aspect involving a degree of indeterminateness or indifference, or involving only aptitude or degree of actuality or something [e.g., the act of generation] that could conceivably have passed away before [paternity] occurred.

4.63 But if you ask: Under what formal aspect would the first person be thought of as incommunicably existing? I reply: Perhaps one could abstract from the very relative incommunicable concept itself or from that absolute incommunicable form, some less specific concept, namely, "this form" or "this incommunicable entity." And then perhaps one could conceive of this, in its proper singularity, to be that by which this person is incommunicable without conceiving anything more specific about his individuality. I do this sort of thing when I conceive not just "being" but "this being" or "this substance" without thinking of this individual in any more specific way, as I do when I view some distant object, seeing it as a body before perceiving it to be an animal or just one animal. And perhaps it is this indifferent concept of an incommunicable form that he had in mind who thought of a divine suppositum without yet determining in his intellect whether the suppositum is absolute or relative. How else could one explain what philosophers thought of God's activity in the world without assuming their every notion false? For it is clear they did not think of this relative suppositum as moving the heavens, yet they did assume some suppositum did so, because every action is ascribed to some suppositum. If they did not think of the notion of an incommunicable suppositum as indifferent to both absolute and relative, then they necessarily thought that this suppositum moving the heavens was absolute, which is false. What we say here about some concept indif-

ferent to both absolute and relative or about that of an incommunicable suppositum unspecified as either absolute or relative is not in any way at odds with our prior statement that
every entity invested with reality is either formally absolute or
formally relative. For one can readily abstract from several
things an indifferent concept, neither relative nor absolute.
Nevertheless everything when specified to be existing
extramentally has to be determinately either one or the other.
Hence indifference of the concept that can be abstracted from
several individuals does not imply a like indifference in the existing individual.

Reading Two
Quodlibet 16, article 2-3, 16.30-16.46
Can Freedom and Necessity Coexist in the Will?[2]

16.30 [Affirmative View] As for the second article, I claim that both freedom and necessity in willing can coexist in the will...

16.31 Reason proves the same point. The first is a proof of simple fact. From the preceding article we know the divine will necessarily wills its own goodness, and yet is free in willing this; therefore [necessity and freedom coexist there]. Proof of the minor: A power or potency that acts with respect to an object, not as something absolute but as related to another, acts with respect to both objects. Thus the Philosopher argues in *On the Soul II, 4* that the faculty by which we know the difference between one object and another is apt by nature to know both objects in themselves. He illustrates this as regards the common or central sense. Now the divine will relates to the end other objects willed for the sake of the end, therefore, as the same basic power, it acts with respect to both. But it acts freely as regards things other than the end, since it wills them contingently. Contingency in acting stems from a principle that is freely, not naturally, active. Therefore, the will as the same basic power wills its own goodness freely.

16.32 Furthermore, there are proofs of the reasoned fact to establish our claim. The first is this: Action that has to do with the ultimate end is the most perfect. But constancy pertains to the perfection of such an action. Therefore, the necessity to be found there does not do away with but rather demands what is needed for perfection, namely, constancy.[3]

Furthermore, an intrinsic condition for a power, considered absolutely or in relation to a perfect act, cannot be opposed to perfection in acting. Now liberty is an intrinsic condition of the will, either considered absolutely or as regards a perfect act. Therefore, liberty can coexist with that condition in acting that is the most perfect possible. Such is necessity, particularly where it is possible to have this. But it is always possible where neither of the extremes [i.e., the subject willing and the object willed] demands contingency in the action between them [i.e., the will-ing]. Such is the case here, as the previous article proved.

16.33 How freedom coexists with necessity: If you ask, how does freedom coexist with necessity, I answer with the Philosopher "Do not seek a reason for things for which no reason can be given for there is no demonstration of the starting point of demonstration." And so I say here: As this proposition, "The divine will wills the divine goodness," is immediate and necessary, for which no reason can be given other than that this will and this goodness are the sort of things they are, so also "The divine will contingently wills the goodness or existence of another." Again no reason can be given except that it is this sort of will and that sort of good, unless we add in general one brief remark that an infinite will must necessarily have an act as regards an infinite object, because this pertains to perfection, and by the same token it does not act necessarily as regards a finite object, because this would imply imperfection. For it is a matter of imperfection to be necessarily determined to what is posterior [i.e., less perfect] and a matter of perfection to be so determined to what is prior [or more perfect] and it implies concomitant perfection to be so determined to what is on a par with it.

16.34 Confirmation: The division of agents into those which act naturally and those which act freely is not the same as the division of agents into those acting necessarily and those acting contingently. For some natural agents act contingently, because their action can be impeded. For like reasons, then, it is possible that some free agent act necessarily without detriment to its freedom.

16.35 [In the production of the Holy Spirit there is both] As for the third main point, it is claimed that in one act of the divine will, namely, the spiration of the Holy Spirit, natural necessity is somehow involved. This should be understood to mean that the will, simply as will, is not the elicitive principle of the notional act whereby something similar in form to the producer is produced. Otherwise in anything where will existed, it would be the principle of an act by which something similar in form was produced, which is false in the case of creatures. The way to understand this claim, then, is that the will, by virtue of the divine nature in which it exists, has a certain "naturality" to produce the notional act, and is thus its elicitive principle.

By the fact that it is rooted in the divine nature or essence, the will has annexed to it a certain natural force. From this "naturality" or natural force working with it, it acquires a certain natural necessity and thus becomes the elicitive principle of the notional act. There is in the essential will-act as ordered to what is supremely loved a necessity of immutability stemming from free will alone. Nevertheless, insofar as the will's activity is ordered to and terminates with the production of the beloved [i.e., the Holy Spirit], a necessity of immutability accrues to it from this "naturality" which has to do solely with the notional act elicited by the will, or rather by the freedom of the will when conjoined with such "naturality."

In addition the point is made that this "naturality" in the will in no way impedes its freedom, nor is it the elicitive principle of the notional act (for that would militate against the freedom of that act). It is rather something consecutive, annexed to the will, something with the assistance of which the will itself by its power as will and as free is able to elicit its notional act, an act it could not elicit apart from such assistance.

The following propositions, then, are necessary in different ways: (1) "God necessarily lives," for he lives by a necessity of nature; (2) "God necessarily understands," – the necessity here has a different basis, for it stems from an intelligible object determining the intellect to know it; (3) "God necessarily produces the Holy Spirit," for he does so by a natural necessity which does not precede but accompanies [the will's act]; (4) "God necessarily loves himself," – here the necessity is a consequence of liberty's infinite [perfection] and there is no necessity of nature involved.

16.36 [Objections] Counter-arguments: Nothing based upon something, it seems, could have additional grounds for its being necessary than that upon which it is based. Neither could there be two reasons for it being necessary whereas the foundation has only one. Otherwise, if the single basis in the foundation were removed, be this possible or not, the one in what is founded would still be there and hence the foundation would still be necessary and nevertheless no necessity remains there. Now, according to some, notional acts are based upon an essential act, and according to all, essential acts are somehow prior to notional acts. Hence it is impossible that the essential act whereby God loves himself has but one necessity stemming from the single ground, viz., the infinity of the liberty, whereas in the act of spiration there be conjoined to this another ground, viz., natural necessity.

16.37 Furthermore, as perfect memory in the appropriate person is the perfect principle for producing a perfect Word, so a perfect will in the appropriate person or persons would seem to be the perfect principle of producing Perfect Love. Therefore, as memory in the Father is the principle of begetting the Son, so will in Father and Son is the principle of spirating the Holy Spirit. Neither does the co-assistance of something in addition to perfect memory and will seem necessary, in the sense that without such assistance the will could never cause the act of spirating nor the memory the act of speaking [the Word].

16.38 On the other hand, if the assistance be understood as that of object to potency, then memory would require such as much as the will. Perhaps it would be needed even more to communicate the nature by their respective acts than it would be needed to make the act necessary. For of these two principles, viz., object and potency, each is a per se reason for the necessity characteristic of the elicitation of these acts. But perhaps each is not per se a perfect reason why the resulting term is consubstantial with the producer, and then it would be true that such assistance to the essential act is not required. For although an object is required for the act, it would not be needed as the source of the communication of its own perfection.

16.39 [Solution] As for this article one could say there is no difficulty here if "nature" be taken broadly insofar as it applies to everything. For in this sense we call "will" nature and we apply the term even to nonbeings when we speak of the nature of negation. In this broad sense, necessity in any being could be called natural. And since the divine will at least has necessarily some volition by virtue of its perfect liberty, this necessity of perfect liberty could be called "natural" in this way.

But a difficulty arises if we take "nature" more strictly, viz., insofar as "nature" and "liberty" are the primary differences of "agent" or "a principle of action." The Philosopher speaks in this fashion in the *Physics* when he divides "cause" into "nature" and "purpose." "Of the former," namely, those things performed for the sake of an end as are all actions of a *per se* cause, "some are in accordance with deliberate intention, others not." And he adds a little later: "Events that are for the sake of something include whatever may be done as the result of thought or of nature." To these two per se causes he reduces the two incidental causes of chance and fortune. He speaks of this distinction again in the *Metaphysics* when he indicates the way rational and irrational powers perform their acts: "As for potencies of the latter kind," – i.e., irrational powers – "when the agent and patient meet in the way appropriate to the potency in question, the one must act and the other be acted upon, but with the former kind of potency" – i.e., the rational –"this is not necessary"– i.e., even if agent and patient meet, it is not necessary that one must act and the other be acted upon. Of this distinction Augustine speaks in *The City of God:* "There is a fortuitous cause, a natural cause, and a voluntary cause." And he explains each.

16.40 This division of "active principle" is expressed by different names not only by different authors but by Aristotle himself as is clear from the *Physics*. After having remarked, "Some are in accordance with deliberate intention, others not," he adds: "as the result of thought or of nature." In the *Metaphysics* he speaks of "rational" and "irrational potencies."

By the three expressions: "not by deliberate intention," "by nature," and "irrational potency," Aristotle understands the active principle we commonly call "nature." By the other three expressions [viz., "by deliberate intention," "as the result of thought," and "rational potency"] he understands the active principle in which intellect and will concur with regard to an extrinsic act.

16.41 But each of these two potencies, taken in itself, has its own way of functioning as a principle. The intellect does so by way of nature [*per modum naturae*]. Hence, in relation to its own act it is nature. Thus the Son in the divine Trinity is produced by way of nature, although the productive principle be "memory." The will, on the other hand, always functions in its own peculiar way, viz., freely. That is why when it concurs with the intellect, as in the production of artifacts, the whole effect is said to be produced freely and intentionally or with deliberation, since the intention is the superior and immediate principle of the extrinsic production. If at times some naturally active power concurs with the will as one of the subordinate potencies we use in acting, the action, insofar as it stems from the natural active principle, is properly speaking "natural." But since the act as a whole falls under the will, we employ the subordinate potency freely and we are said to act freely by virtue of the higher power. In this way Aristotle speaks in the *Metaphysics* where he wants to introduce some determining factor besides intellect, such as desire or conscious force. Otherwise the intellect would produce simultaneously contrary effects, for knowledge itself at once reveals contrary effects and insofar as itself is concerned, it would be a principle that acts naturally and would cause necessarily everything to which it is in potency: "The rational potencies produce contrary effects, so that if they produce their effects necessarily, they would produce contrary effects at the same time. But this is impossible. There must be, then, something else that decides," – i.e., something that determines the potency to one of the contraries. And he adds: "I mean by this 'desire' or 'conscious choice'. "

16.42 [Conclusion] As for our proposal, I say that even if in the will's action some principle might concur (the object, according to some; the intellect, according to others) and would do so as naturally active, so far as itself is concerned, the will *per se* is never an active principle that acts naturally. To be naturally

active and to be freely active represents a primary division of
"active principle." The will is a freely active principle, which is
precisely why it is called "will." It can no more be naturally active than nature, as other than will, can be freely active.

16.43 But here the question arises: Why is it that the will,
although it acts necessarily, does not act naturally, since nature
could no more determine it to act than does the fact that it has
to act?

Answer: Every natural agent either is first in an absolute
sense, or if not, it will be naturally determined to act by some
prior agent. Now the will can never be an agent that is first in
an absolute sense. But neither can it be naturally determined
by a higher agent, for it is active in such a way that it determines itself to action in the sense that if the will wills something necessarily, for example, A, this volition of A would not be
caused naturally by that which causes the will even if the will
itself were caused naturally, but once the first act by which the
will is caused be given, if the will were left to itself and could
have or not have this volition contingently, it would still determine itself to this volition.

16.44 To the claim, then, that a natural principle cannot be
more determined than a necessary principle, I say: Although
the necessary be most determined in the sense that it excludes
any in-determination as regards an alternative, nevertheless
one necessary thing may in some way be more determined than
another. That fire be hot or the heavens be round is determined
by the cause which produced simultaneously the being of the
heavens and its shape. A weight, on the other hand, is determined to descend. Still it does not receive from its progenitor
the act of descending, but only that principle which naturally
causes it to descend. But if the caused will necessarily wills
anything, it is not determined by its cause to will such in the
way the weight is determined to descend. All it receives from
the cause is a principle by which it determines itself to this volition.

16.45 You might object, if the descent is caused by the body's intrinsic heaviness, then the heavy body moves itself. But why then is it not just as free as a will moving itself to a volition which it causes necessarily?

To this I answer: Causation by gravity is natural whereas the will's causation is free, and the reason is the will is a will and the weight is a weight.

16.46 To put it briefly then, like a form and its mode of being, so an action and the mode of acting are inseparable. Just as there is no reason why this being has this mode of being except that it is that sort of thing, so also there is no reason why this agent has this mode of action (i.e., free, though necessary) except that it is that sort of active principle.

Reading Three
Ordinatio IV, distinction 46.
Divine Justice[4]

Not by way of disparaging these distinctions, I reply with greater brevity to the question that in God there is but one justice, both conceptually and in reality, although by stretching the meaning of "justice" one could say that in addition to the aforesaid justice there is some justice, or rather something just, about the way he deals with creatures.

To explain the first: justice properly speaking represents a habitual state of rectitude of will, and hence as a habit it inclines one in a quasi-natural manner to another or to oneself as quasi-other. Now, the divine will does not have any rectitude that would incline it deterministically to anything other than its own goodness as a quasi-other (recall that the divine will is related to any other object only contingently, so that as will it has the capacity to will either this or its opposite). From this it follows that there is no justice in God except that which inclines him to render to his own goodness what is its due.

Thus there is also but one act, conceptually and in reality, to which this habit of justice inclines this will. Nevertheless this will-act, in terms of what follows from it, has to do with many secondary objects... that the divine intellect, in addition to its one primary object and act, regards a multiplicity of secondary objects. There is a difference, however, between the intellect there and the will here, because the divine intellect of necessity regards these secondary objects, whereas here the will regards its secondary objects only in a contingent manner. And hence not only is it the case that both there and here neither act depends upon its respective secondary objects, but here the will is not necessarily related to its secondary objects in the way the intellect necessarily knows its secondary objects.

But if we wish to distinguish this one real will-act into many conceptually distinct acts, just as there we distinguish one real intellection into many conceptually distinct acts of knowledge insofar as it has to do with a multiplicity of secondary objects, I say that where the will-act is concerned one cannot even speak of conceptually quasi distinct "justices." In fact we cannot even speak of one justice as regards these multiple secondary objects, howsoever that justice might be distinct or indistinct. The reason is that a habit inclines after the manner of nature and thus limits the respective faculty to but one mode of action, so that it would be repugnant for a potency having such a habit to tend towards the opposite. But there is nothing in the, divine will that inclines it specifically to any secondary object in such a way that it would be impossible for it justly to incline towards it opposite. For without contradiction the will could will the opposite and thus it could justly will such; otherwise it could will something absolutely [i.e., by its absolute power] and not do so justly, which seems incongruous.

And this is what Anselm says in ch. 11 of his *Proslogion*: "Only what you will is just, and only what you do not will is not just." As such, if one postulates in the divine intellect some intellective habit with respect to oneself and to others, one could make a stronger case for a conceptual distinction than in the case at hand, because there the intellect is deterministically inclined to each of the secondary objects, but that is not the case here with the will. Nevertheless, one could say that this single justice, which determinately inclines the divine will to its first act, modifies each of these secondary acts, although not in a necessary manner, as though it could not also modify the opposite of each. Neither does this justice precede the will, as it were, inclining it after the manner of nature to some secondary act; but the will first determines itself in regard to each secondary object. And by this very fact this act is modified by that first justice, because that act is in harmony with the will to which it is conformed as if the rectitude inclining it this way were the first justice itself.

In this second way God is said to do what is right in a creature from the way he makes one created thing correspond to another (just as we say it is just on the part of the creature that fire be hot and water cold, that fire rise and water descend, and so on), because this created nature demands this as something suited to it – just as we could say in politics that while justice exists as such only in the ruler himself, we could still speak of him as being somehow just in the things he ordains, namely, to the extent that he arranges things in such and such a way, since this is something demanded by the things themselves insofar as they are destined by nature for the use of the citizens.

However, the primary justice intrinsic to God does not determine him to be just in this second way in the same manner that it determines him in regard to his first act, because this primary act [of justice towards himself] does not look to any [created] object or secondary act, because insofar as it looks to such his justice does not incline his justice does not incline his will in any necessary manner, as was said.

Readings Four/Five
Ordinatio IV, distinction 15.
Private Property
Social Contract Theory[5]

ARTICLE I. THE SOURCE OF DISTINCT PROPERTY RIGHTS

As for the first question, the first conclusion is this: "In the state of innocence neither divine nor natural law provided for distinct ownership of property; on the contrary everything was common." Proof is found in [Gratian's] *Decrees* [dist. 8, ch. 1]: "By the law of nature all things are common to all," where he cites Augustine's commentary on the Gospel of John: "By what law do you defend the real estate of the Church? Is it divine or human? The first is found in the divine Scriptures, the human we have from the law of kings. Whence do we possess what we possess? Is it not by human law? For by divine law 'the earth and the fullness thereof is the Lord's.' And is not the reason the earth bears both poor and rich the will of man? It is by human law, therefore, that we say: 'This house is mine, this farm is mine, this servant is mine." Again in the same place Augustine says: "Remove the Emperor's laws and who will dare say: 'This is my farm'?" And later, in the same work, he adds: "By the king's laws we own our possessions." And in [Gratian's *Decrees*] *Causa* 12, q. 1, *Dilectissimis*: "All men ought to have the common use of everything on earth."

The rationale for this is twofold. According to right reason men should have the use of things in such a way as, first, to contribute to a peaceful and decent life, and [second] to provide needed sustenance. But in the state of innocence common use with no distinct ownership would have been more conducive to this than individual ownership, for no one would have taken what another needed, nor would the latter have had to wrest it by force from the other; rather each would have taken what first came to hand as needed for that persons' use. In this way also a greater sufficiency for sustenance would have obtained than if one person's use of a thing were precluded because another had monopolized it.

Our second conclusion is this: "After the Fall of man, this law of nature of holding all things in common was revoked."

This also was reasonable, for the same two reasons. First of all communality of all property would have militated against the peaceful life. For the evil and covetous person would take more than needed and to do so, would also use violence against others who wished to use these common goods for their own needs, as we read of Nimrod, the first potentate: "He was a mighty hunter before the Lord!" – that is to say he was an oppressor of men. Secondly, the original law would also have failed to ensure the necessary sustenance of mankind, for those stronger and more belligerent would have deprived the others of necessities. Therefore, the commonwealth Aristotle describes in Bk. II of the *Politics*, wherein all things were not held in common, was much better than that of Socrates, which Aristotle rejected because of the condition in which he found man to exist.

The third conclusion is this: "Once this natural law precept of having all in common was revoked, and thus permission was given to appropriate and divide up what had been common, there was still no actual division imposed either by natural or by divine law."

Not by divine law, as the aforesaid citation from Augustine proves –"By what law?" and so on. Not by a law of nature, in all probability. For nothing indicates that the original law was reversed rather than revoked (and the original determination of the law was that all things be common), unless we take to be natural law the proposition in *The Enactments of Justinian*: "Whatever formerly belonged to no one is conceded by natural reason to the first person obtaining possession of the same." For even though it seems clear that, in all probability, a division must take place once natural reason grasped that goods should be divided, it seems more plausible to say this was effected by positive law rather than the law of nature. It would follow from this that the first division of property was brought about by some positive legislation. To see why this division was just therefore, we must consider why such a positive law would be just.

Hence, we have this fourth conclusion: "What a just positive law requires of its legislator is prudence and authority."

Prudence, that he might dictate what ought to be established for the community according to practical right reason. Authority, because "law" is derived from a verb that means "to bind," and not every judgment of a prudent man binds the community, or binds any person if the man is head of nothing. It is clear enough how prudence could have been operative in figuring out just laws. But what of the just authority required if the law is to be just?

THE ORIGIN OF CIVIL AUTHORITY

A fifth conclusion follows: "Authority or rulership takes two forms, paternal and political. And political authority is twofold, that vested in one person and that vested in a group." – The first, namely, paternal authority, is just by natural law in virtue of which children are bound to obey their parents. Neither was this revoked by any positive Mosaic or Gospel law, but rather it was confirmed. – Political authority, however, which-is exercised over those outside [the family], whether it resides in one person or in a community, can be just by common consent and election on the part of the community.

The first [or parental sort of] authority regards natural descendants, even though they do not dwell in the same city, whereas the second has to do with those who live together even though there is no consanguinity or close relationship between them. Thus, if some outsiders banded together to build a city or live in one, seeing that they could not be well governed without some form of authority, they could have amicably agreed to commit their community to one person or to a group, and if to one person, to him alone and to a successor who would be chosen as he was, or to him and his posterity. And both of these forms of political authority are just, because one person can justly submit himself to another or to a community in those things which are not against the law of God and as regards which he can be guided better by the person or persons to whom he has submitted or subjected himself than he could by himself. Hence, we have here all that is required to pass a just law, because it would be promulgated by one who possesses prudence either in himself or in his counselors and enjoys authority in one of the several ways mentioned in this conclusion.

From this the sixth conclusion follows: "The first division of ownership could have been just by reason of some just positive law passed by the father or the regent ruling justly or by a community ruling or regulating justly, and this is probably how it was done."

For after the flood, Noah divided the earth among his sons, each of which occupied a portion for himself and did the same for his sons and posterity, or else the latter divided it further by common agreement, as we read in Genesis 13 about Abraham and Lot, for Abraham gave Lot his choice and took what remained for himself. Or a law could have been promulgated by a father or by someone elected as ruler or by a group to whom the community gave this authority. This law, I say, was or could have been that anything unclaimed would go to the first occupant, and then they split up and fanned out over the face of the earth, one occupying this area, another that.

Notes

[1]John Duns Scotus, *God and Creatures: The Quodlibetal Questions*, trans. with an introduction, notes and glossary by Felix Alluntis and Allan B. Wolter (Princeton, NJ: Princeton University Press, 1975), 103-105. Reprinted with permission.

[2]John Duns Scotus, *God and Creatures: The Quodlibetal Questions*, trans. with an introduction, notes and glossary by Felix Alluntis and Allan B. Wolter (Princeton, NJ: Princeton University Press, 1975), 377-384. Reprinted with permission.

[3]I have altered this text in light of William Frank's reading of *firmitas* rather than *libertas* in this passage. See his "Duns Scotus's Concept of Willing Freely," p. 80, note 20.

[3]Allan B. Wolter, *Duns Scotus on the Will and Morality* (Washington, D.C.: Catholic University of America Press, 1986) 245-249; 1997 edition: 186-188. Reprinted with permission.

[4]John Duns Scotus, *Political and Economic Philosophy*, trans. With an introduction and notes by Allan B. Wolter (St. Bonaventure, NY: The Franciscan Institute, 2001), 29-35.

Bibliography

I. General Bibliography

Aertsen, Jan A. "Beauty in the Middle Ages: A Forgotten Transcendental?" *Medieval Philosophy and Theology* 1 (1991): 68-97.

Barth, Timothy. "Being, Univocity and Analogy According to Duns Scotus." In *John Duns Scotus, 1265-1965,* eds. John K. Ryan, and Bernardine Bonansea, 210-62. Washington: Catholic University of America Press, 1965.

Bettoni, Efrem. "The Originality of the Scotistic Synthesis." In *John Duns Scotus: 1265-1965*, eds. John K. Ryan and Bernardine Bonansea, 28-44. Washington: Catholic University of America Press, 1965.

———. *Duns Scotus: Basic Principles of His Philosophy.* Washington: Catholic University of America Press, 1961.

Boler, John. "Transcending the Natural: Duns Scotus on the Two Affections of the Will." *American Catholic Philosophical Quarterly* 67 (1993): 109-126.

Bonansea, Bernardine. *Man and his Approach to God in John Duns Scotus*. Lanham, MD: University Press of America, 1983.

Boulnois, Olivier. *"Duns Scot, théoricien de l'analogie de l'être."* In *John Duns Scotus: Metaphysics and Ethics,* eds. Ludger Honnefelder, Rega Wood, Mechtild Dreyer, 293-315. Leiden: Brill, 1996.

Cross, Richard. *Duns Scotus*, New York: Oxford University Press, 1999.

Dumont, Richard. "Intuition: Prescript or Postscript to Scotus's Demonstration of God's Existence." *Deus et Homo ad mentem I. Duns Scoti*, 81-7. Rome: Cura Commissionis Scotisticae, 1972.

Dumont, Stephen. "The Question on Individuation in Scotus's *Quaestiones super Metaphysicam."* In *Via Scoti: Methodologica ad mentem Joannis Duns Scoti,* ed. Leonardo Sileo, 193-228. Rome: Edizione Antonianum, 1995.

———. "Theology as a Science and Duns Scotus's Distinction between Intuitive and Abstractive Cognition." *Speculum* 64 (1989): 579-99.

Frank, William. "Duns Scotus's Concept of Willing Freely: What Divine Freedom Beyond Choice Teaches Us." *Franciscan Studies* 42 (1982): 68-89.

Ghisalberti, Alessandro. "Ens Infinitum e dimonstrazione dell'esistenza di Dio in Duns Scoto." In *John Duns Scotus: Metaphysics and Ethics,* eds. Ludger Honnefelder, Rega Wood, Mechtild Dreyer, 415-434. Leiden: Brill, 1996.

Ingham, Mary B. "Duns Scotus, Morality and Happiness: A Reply to Thomas Williams." *American Catholic Philosophical Quarterly* 74.2 (2000): 173-95.

———. "The Condemnation of 1277: Another Light on Scotist Ethics." *Freiburger Zeitschrift für Theologie und Philosophie* 37 (1990): 91-103.

———. *"Ea Quae Sunt ad Finem*: Reflections on Virtue as a Means to Moral Excellence in Scotist Thought." *Franciscan Studies* 50 (1990): 177-95.

_____. "Scotus and the Moral Order." *American Catholic Philosophical Quarterly* 67 (1993): 127-50.

_____. "Duns Scotus: Moral Reasoning and the Artistic Paradigm." In *Via Scoti: Methodologica ad mentem Joannis Duns Scoti,* ed. Leonardo Sileo, 825-837. Rome: Edizioni Antonianum, 1995.

_____. *The Harmony of Goodness: Mutuality and Moral Living According to John Duns Scotus.* Quincy, IL: Franciscan Press, 1996.

_____. "Letting Scotus Speak for Himself." *Medieval Philosophy and Theology* 10.2 (2001): 173-216.

Kovach, Francis. "Divine and Human Beauty in Duns Scotus's Philosophy and Theology." In *Deus et Homo ad Mentem I. Duns Scoti*, 445-459. Rome: Cura Commissionis Scotisticae, 1972.

Lottin, Odon. *Psychologie et morale aux 12e et 13e siècles.* Volume IV. Louvain: Gembloux, 1954.

Noone, Timothy. "Scotus's Critique of the Thomistic Theory of Individuation and the Dating of the *Quaestiones Super Libros Metaphysicorum."VII.* In *Via Scoti:Methodologica ad mentem Joannis Duns Scoti,* ed. Leonardo Sileo, 391-406. Rome: Edizione Antonianum, 1995.

Normore, Calvin G. "Scotus, Modality, Instants of Nature and the Contingency of the Present." In *John Duns Scotus: Metaphysics and Ethics*, eds. Ludger Honnefelder, Rega Wood, Mechtild Dreyer, 161-174. Leiden: Brill 1996.

North, R. "The Scotist Cosmic Christ." In *De Doctrina I. Duns Scoti,* Vol. 3: 169-212. Rome: Cura Commissionis Scotisticae, 1968.

O'Connor, Timothy. "From First Efficient Cause to God: Scotus on the Identification Stage of the Cosmological Argument." In *John Duns Scotus: Metaphysics and Ethics,* eds. Ludger Honnefelder, Rega Wood, Mechtild Dreyer, 435-454. Leiden: Brill, 1996.

Prentice, Robert. "The Contingent Element Governing the Natural Law on the Last Seven Precepts of the Decalogue, According to Duns Scotus." *Antonianum* 42 (1967): 259-92.

Vignaux, P. "Infini, Liberté et Histoire de salut." In *Deus et Homo ad Mentem I. Duns Scoti*, 495-507. Rome: Cura Commissionis Scotisticae, 1972.

_____. "Lire Duns Scot Aujourd'hui." *Regnum hominis et Regnum Dei*, 33-46. Rome: Cura Commissionis Scotisticae, 1976.

_____. "Valeur morale et valeur de salut" *Homo et Mundus*, 53-67. Rome: Cura Commissionis Scotisticae, 1984.

Wieland, Georg. "The Reception of Aristotle's Ethics." In *The Cambridge History of Later Medieval Philosophy*, eds. Anthony Kenny, Norman Kretzmann, Jan Pinborg, 657-72. Cambridge: Cambridge University Press, 1982.

_____. "Happiness, The Perfection of Man." In *The Cambridge History of Later Medieval Philosophy*, eds. Anthony Kenny, Norman Kretzmann, Jan Pinborg, 673-86. Cambridge: Cambridge University Press, 1982.

Williams, T. "How Scotus Separates Morality from Happiness." *American Catholic Philosopical Quarterly* (1995): 425-445.

Wolter, Allan B. "Reflections about Scotus's Early Works." In *John Duns Scotus: Metaphysics and Ethics*, eds. Ludger Honnefelder, Rega Wood, Mechtil Dreyer, 37-58. Leiden: Brill, 1996.

_____. "The Formal Distinction." In *The Philosophical Theology of John Duns Scotus*, ed. Marilyn McCord Adams, 27-41. Ithaca: Cornell University Press, 1990.

_____. "Duns Scotus on Intuition, Memory and our Knowledge of Individuals," In *The Philosophical Theology of John Duns Scotus.*, ed. Marilyn McCord Adams, 98-122. Ithaca: Cornell University Press, 1990.

_____. "Scotus's Individuation Theory." In *The Philosophical Theology of John Duns Scotus,* ed. Marilyn McCord Adams, 68-97. Ithaca: Cornell University Press, 1990.

_____. *Four Questions on Mary.* St. Bonaventure, NY: The Franciscan Institute, 2001.

_____. "Duns Scotus on the Primacy and Personality of Christ." In *Franciscan Christology,* ed. Damian McElrath, 139-182. St. Bonaventure, NY: The Franciscan Institute. Franciscan Sources, No. 1, 1980, 1994.

_____. "The Doctrine of the Immaculate Conception in the Early Franciscan School." *Studia Mariana* 9. Franciscan National Marian Commission 1954: 48-58.

_____. "Native Freedom of the Will as a Key to the Ethics of Scotus." In *The Philosophical Theology of John Duns Scotus*, ed. Marilyn McCord Adams, 148-62. Ithaca: Cornell University Press, 1990.

_____. "Duns Scotus on the Natural Desire for the Supernatural." In *The Philosophical Theology of John Duns Scotus,* ed. Marilyn McCord Adams, 125-47. Ithaca: Cornell University Press, 1990.

Wood, Rega. "Scotus's Argument for the Existence of God." *Franciscan Studies* 47 (1987): 257-78.

Zavalloni, Roberto. "Personal Freedom and Scotus' Voluntarism." In *De Doctrina I. Duns Scoti,*Vvol. 2: 613-27. Rome: Cura Commissionis Scotisticae, 1968.

II. Further Readings

CHAPTER 1

On the historical context:

Brampton, Charles K. "Duns Scotus at Oxford, 1288-1301." *Franciscan Studies* 24 (1964): 5-20.

Courtney, W. "Scotus at Paris." In *Via Scoti: Methodologica ad mentem Joannis Duns Scoti,* ed. Leonardo Sileo, 149-164. Rome: Edizione Antonianum, 1995.

Ingham, Mary B. "Duns Scotus, Morality and Happiness: A Reply to Thomas Williams." *American Catholic Philosophical Quarterly* 74.2 (2000): 173-195.

_____. "The Condemnation of 1277: Another Light on Scotist Ethics." *Freiburger Zeitschrift für Theologie und Philosophie* 37 (1990): 91-103.

Roest, Bert. *A History of Franciscan Education (1210-1517).* Leiden: Brill, 2000.

Wieland, Georg. "The Reception of Aristotle's Ethics." In *The Cambridge History of Later Medieval Philosophy*, eds. Anthony Kenny, Norman Kretzmann, Jan Pinborg, 657-72. Cambridge: Cambridge University Press, 1982.

_____. "Happiness, The Perfection of Man." In *The Cambridge History of Later Medieval Philosophy*, eds. Anthony Kenny, Norman Kretzmann, Jan Pinborg, 673-686. Cambridge: Cambridge University Press, 1982.

Wolter, Allan B.. "Reflections about Scotus's Early Works." In *John Duns Scotus: Metaphysics and Ethics*, eds. Ludger Honnefelder, Rega Wood, Mechtild Dreyer, 37-58. Leiden: Brill, 1996.

CHAPTER 2

On contingency and the existence of God:

Ghisalberti, Alessandro. "Ens Infinitum e dimonstrazione dell'esistenza di Dio in Duns Scoto." In *John Duns Scotus: Metaphysics and Ethics*, eds. Ludger Honnefelder, Rega Wood, Mechtild Dreyer, 415-434. Leiden: Brill, 1996.

Normore, Calvin. "Scotus, Modality, Instants of Nature and the Contingency of the Present." In *John Duns Scotus: Metaphysics and Ethics*, eds. Ludger Honnefelder, Rega Wood, Mechtild Dreyer, 161-174. Leiden: Brill, 1996.

O'Connor, Timothy. "From First Efficient Cause to God: Scotus on the Identification Stage of the Cosmological Argument." In *John Duns Scotus: Metaphysics and Ethics*, eds. Ludger Honnefelder, Rega Wood, Mechtild Dreyer, 435-454. Leiden: Brill, 1996.

Wood, Rega. "Scotus's Argument for the Existence of God." *Franciscan Studies* 47 (1987): 257-78.

On individuation:

Dumont, Stephen. "The Question on Individuation in Scotus's *Quaestiones super Metaphysicam.*" In *Via Scoti*, In *Via Scoti: Methodologica ad mentem Joannis Duns Scoti*, ed. Leonardo Sileo, 193-228. Rome: Edizione Antonianum, 1995.

Noone, Timothy. "Scotus's Critique of the Thomistic Theory of Individuation and the Dating of the *Quaestiones Super Libros Metaphysicorum*, VII, 13." In *Via Scoti: Methodologica ad mentem Joannis Duns Scoti*, ed. Leonardo Sileo, 391-406. Rome: Edizione Antonianum, 1995.

Wolter, Allan B. "Scotus's Individuation Theory." In *The Philosophical Theology of John Duns Scotus*, ed. Marilyn M. Adams, 68-97. Ithaca: Cornell University Press, 1990.

On cognition and the univocity of being:

Barth, Timothy. "Being, Univocity and Analogy According to Duns Scotus." In *John Duns Scotus, 1265-1965*, eds. John K. Ryan, and Bernardine Bonansea, 210-262. Washington: Catholic University Press, 1965.

Boulnois, Olivier. "Duns Scot, théoricien de l'analogie de l'être." In *John Duns Scotus: Metaphysics and Ethics,* eds. Ludger Honnefelder, Rega Wood, Mechtild Dreyer, 293-315. Leiden: Brill, 1996.

Dumont, Richard. "Intuition: Prescript or Postscript to Scotus's Demonstration of God's Existence." In *Deus et Homo ad mentem I. Duns Scoti*, 81-87. Rome: Cura Commissionis Scotisticae, 1972.

Dumont, Stephen. "Theology as a Science and Duns Scotus's Distinction between Intuitive and Abstractive Cognition." *Speculum* 64 (1989): 579-599.

Wolter, Allan B. "The Formal Distinction." In *The Philosophical Theology of John Duns Scotus*, ed. Marilyn M. Adams, 27-41. Ithaca: Cornell University Press, 1990.

_____. "Duns Scotus on Intuition, Memory and our Knowledge of Individuals." In *The Philosophical Theology of John Duns Scotus,* ed. Marilyn M. Adams, 98-124. Ithaca: Cornell University Press, 1990.

CHAPTER 3

On the Incarnation:

Bonansea, Bernardino. *Man and his Approach to God in John Duns Scotus*. Lanham, MD: University Press of America, 1983.

Bettoni, Efrem. "The Originality of the Scotistic Synthesis." In *John Duns Scotus, 1265-1965,* eds. John K. Ryan, and Bernardine Bonansea, 28-44. Washington: Catholic University Press, 1965.

North, Robert. "The Scotist Cosmic Christ." In *De Doctrina I. Duns Scoti* Rome: Cura Commissionis Scotisticae, 1968, Vol. 3: 169-212.

Vignaux, Paul. "Infini, Liberté et Histoire de salut." In *Deus et Homo ad Mentem I. Duns Scoti*, 495-507. Rome: Cura Commissionis Scotisticae, 1972

Wolter, Allan B. "Introduction" in *Four Questions on Mary*, 1-18. St. Bonaventure: The Franciscan Institute, 2001.

_____. "Duns Scotus on the Primacy and Personality of Christ." In *Franciscan Christology,* ed. Damian McElrath, 139-182. St. Bonaventure: The Franciscan Institute. Franciscan Sources, No. 1, 1980, 1994.

On the Immaculate Conception:

Brady, Ignatius. "The Development of the Doctrine of the Immaculate Conception in the Fourteenth Century After Aureoli." *Franciscan Studies* 15 (1955): 175-202.

Lottin, Odon. *Psychologie et morale aux 12e et 13e siècles*. Vol. IV, part 3, 11-280. Louvain: Gembloux, 1954.

Mildner, Francis M. "The Immaculate Conception in England up to the Time of John Duns Scotus," *Marianum* 1 (1939), 86-99, 200-221; 2 (1940), 173-193; 284-306.

Vogt, Berard. "Duns Scotus, Defender of the Immaculate Conception: An Historical-Dogmatic Study." *Studia Mariana* 9 (1954): 161-175.

Wolter, Allan B. "Introduction" in *Four Questions on Mary*, 1-18. St. Bonaventure: Franciscan Institute Press, 2001.

_____. "Doctrine of the Immaculate Conception in the Early Franciscan School." *Studia Mariana* 9, 48-58. Franciscan National Marian Commission, 1954.

On Moral theory:

Aertsen, Jan A. "Beauty in the Middle Ages: A Forgotten Transcendental? *Medieval Philosophy and Theology* 1 (1991): 68-97.

Bettoni, Efrem. *Duns Scotus: Basic Principles of His Philosophy*. Washington: Catholic University of America: 1961.

Boler, John. "Transcending the Natural: Duns Scotus on the Two Affections of the Will." *American Catholic Philosophical Quarterly* 67 (1993): 109-126.

Ingham, Mary B. "*Ea Quae Sunt ad Finem*: Reflections on Virtue as a Means to Moral Excellence in Scotist Thought." *Franciscan Studies* 50 (1990): 177-195.

_____. "Scotus and the Moral Order." *American Catholic Philosophical Quarterly* 67 (1993): 127-150.

_____. "Duns Scotus: Moral Reasoning and the Artistic Paradigm." *Via Scoti*, 825-837.

_____. "Duns Scotus, Morality and Happiness: A Reply to Thomas Williams." *ACPQ* 74 (2000): 173-195.

_____. "Letting Scotus Speak for Himself." *Medieval Philosophy and Theology* 10, 2 (2001): 173-216.

_____. "Did Scotus Modify His Position on the Relationship of Intellect and Will?" *Recherches de Théologie et Philosophie médiévales* 69.1 (2002): 88-116.

Kovach, Francis. "Divine and Human Beauty in Duns Scotus's Philosophy and Theology." In *Deus et Homo ad Mentem I. Duns Scoti*, 445-459. Rome: Cura Commissionis Scotisticae, 1972.

Prentice, Robert. "The Contingent Element Governing the Natural Law on the Last Seven Precepts of the Decalogue, According to Duns Scotus." *Antonianum* 42 (1967): 259-292.

Vignaux, Paul. "Valeur morale et valeur de salut." *Homo et Mundus*, 53-67. Rome: Cura Commissionis Scotisticae, 1984.

Wolter, Allan B. "Native Freedom of the Will as a Key to the Ethics of Scotus." In *The Philosophical Theology of John Duns Scotus,* ed. Marilyn M. Adams, 148-162. Ithaca: Cornell University Press, 1990.

_____. "Duns Scotus on the Natural Desire for the Supernatural." *The Philosophical Theology of John Duns Scotus,* ed. Marilyn M. Adams, 125-147. Ithaca: Cornell University Press, 1990..

Zavalloni, Roberto. "Personal Freedom and Scotus' Voluntarism." *De Doctrina I. Duns Scoti*, vol. 2: 613-627.

CHAPTER 4

Frank, William. "Duns Scotus's Concept of Willing Freely: What Divine Freedom Beyond Choice Teaches Us." *Franciscan Studies* 42 (1982): 68-89.

Gandillac, Maurice de. "Loi naturelle et fondements de l'ordre social selon les principes du B. Duns Scot." *De Doctrina I. Duns Scoti*, II: 683-734. Rome: Cura Commissionis Scotisticae, 1968.

Ingham, Mary B. "John Duns Scotus: An Integrated Vision." *The History of Franciscan Theology*, ed. Kenan Osborne, O.F.M., 185-230. St. Bonaventure NY: The Franciscan Institute, 1994.

_____. *The Harmony of Goodness: Mutuality and Moral Living According to John Duns Scotus*. Quincy: Franciscan Press, 1996.

CHAPTER 5

On the contemporary relevance of Scotist thought:

Beraud de St-Maurice. "The Contemporary Significance of Duns Scotus's Philosophy." In *John Duns Scotus, 1265-1965*, eds. John K. Ryan, and Bernardine Bonansea, 185-230. Washington: Catholic University Press, 1965.

Bos, Egbert.P. *John Duns Scotus and the Renewal of Philosophy*. Amsterdam/Atlanta: Radophi, 1998.

Osborne, Kenan. "John Duns Scotus in the Postmodern, Scientific World." In *The Franciscan Intellectual Tradition*, ed. Elise Saggau, O.S.F., 57-82. St. Bonaventure, NY: Franciscan Institute Publications, 2002.

Vignaux, Paul. "Lire Duns Scot Aujourd'hui." *Regnum hominis et Regnum Dei*, 33-46. Rome: Cura Commissionis Scotisticae, 1976.

GLOSSARY

Abstractive cognition – The act by which the mind knows reality via sense perception. Abstraction is a mediated cognitive act that does not admit of certainty. It considers the object independently of its existence or non-existence. Based upon Aristotle's discussion of knowing in *De Anima* III, 5, such cognition was understood to involve various stages of sense perception, imaginary phantasms and, finally, abstract concepts that reveal the extra-mental world to the knower.

Acceptatio – The divine act of delight or acceptance, by which the morally good act, when informed by charity, is rewarded by God.

Accidentally ordered causes – Distinct from causes that are essentially ordered, a series or concatenation of causes, such as a sequence of events or a series of generative causes (grandparents, parents, child), which produce a final effect. No member of the series depends upon an earlier member for its causal activity. These were the sorts of causes analyzed by Hume.

Affection for justice (affectio iustitiae) – Originally from Anselm, this represents the highest moral disposition in the will. It is that disposition whereby the will is drawn to love the good because of its intrinsic value (see *goods of value*), and not because of any personal gain. For Scotus, this affection constitutes the will's native freedom or innate liberty; it was not lost after the Fall. This disposition is perfected by charity.

Affection for possession/happiness (affectio commodi) – Also from Anselm, this represents the natural disposition toward self-protection and perfection in every living being. In the will, this is the disposition whereby the will is drawn to love goods that bring pleasure and enjoyment to the self. It is a self-directed disposition that is perfected by hope.

Agent intellect (intellectus agens) – Based upon the difficult passage of Aristotle's *De Anima* III, 5, this term refers to the active role of the intellect in understanding reality based upon sense perception. In the Augustinian tradition, the agent intellect was identified with God. Arab thinkers identified it with an intelligence or angel located at the level of the moon. Aquinas located it within the soul, but considered it really distinct from the possible intellect. Both active (agent) and passive (possible) intellects work to give birth to the conceptual order. This order is distinct from, but dependent upon, sense knowledge. Scotus understands the agent intellect to be a faculty of the soul, identical to but formally distinct from the possible intellect. The agent intellect renders intelligible what is potentially knowable in the sense image (or phantasm).

Book of Sentences – Foundational textbook used for scholastic education. Authored by Peter Lombard, a student of logician Peter Abelard (1079-1142), the *Book of Sentences* contains a doctrinal compendium of the truths of Catholic faith, organized in question/answer format. Each bachelor was required to lecture on the Book of Sentences as part of his educational training.

Causality, free – The order of free causality refers to the action of the cause that is rational, or capable of self-movement and self-restraint. The will alone belongs to the order of free causality.

Causality, necessary or natural – The order of necessary causality refers to the action of those causes that are determined to produce an effect, unless prevented or hindered by someone or something external to them. The intellect belongs to the order of necessary causality.

Contingency – The order of contingency refers to those beings that can exist but do not need to exist. In the case of an actually existing being or state of affairs, contingency refers to the fact that it might not have existed or not in this particular way.

Divine action ad extra – Action external to the Trinity of persons. Everything here is contingent.

Divine action ad intra – Action internal to the Trinity of persons. Everything here is necessary (or natural).

Divine foreknowledge – God's knowledge of future events. Scotus holds that God knows future events through the divine will.

Ens, ens commune – Literally *being, common being,* the first object of the intellect.

Essentially ordered causes – In an essentially ordered series of causes, all causes must coexist to produce and conserve the effect. Such causes can be of different types (formal, final, material, efficient) or within a chain of the same type (efficient causes). In the case of an essential order, no infinite regress is possible. The chain as a whole must be essentially ordered to some coexisting cause that grounds the order. Such an ordering is especially important in Scotus's argument for God's existence.

Firmitas – Steadfastness or fidelity. The characteristic of the divine will where freedom and necessity coincide. See *Quodlibet* 16.

Formal distinction, formality – At a midpoint between a conceptual distinction (only in the mind) and a real distinction (capable of independent existence outside the mind), the formal distinction (or formal non-identity) refers to potentially knowable aspects of a given reality (*a parte rei*) that do not exist independently of the object in question. For Scotus, the intellect and will are formally distinct, since knowing is not willing, yet both are one in the person. The formal distinction enables Scotus to deal with the Trinity of Persons in God, along with the divine perfections, without sacrificing divine simplicity.

Free choice, synchronic – The power for opposites in the same instant. Scotus refers to the ability of the divine will to retain freedom of choice (*de potentia absoluta*) even after an alternative is chosen (*de potentia ordinata*). This guarantees the absolute contingency of the present as it relates to the divine will. The human will also has this sort of freedom, in the sense that at a given moment, the will can will a or ~a.

Free will – The will's capacity as an active potency to determine itself in opposite ways.

Freedom – The order of causality that includes and explains the will's ability to control and determine itself as well as the ability of the will to choose rectitude for its own sake (the perfection of the affection for justice). In Scotist thought, freedom explains why the will is independent from causal factors external to itself (its indetermination) and why it possesses the capacity for self-direction (its self-determination). Freedom also refers to the fullness of perfection in divine creative activity. In God, freedom and necessity coincide.

***Goods of use (bonum utile*)** – Goods whose worth is derived from their use.

Goods of value (bonum honestum) – Goods of intrinsic worth.

Haecceitas – From *haec* (literally *this*); the individuating principle of each being; the ultimate reality of the being.

Hylomorphism – Literally matter (*hyle*) and form (*morphe*), this refers to the Aristotelian theory of substances. Every substance is composed of both matter and form.

Imputability – When an act lies in the power of an agent, the act is imputable to the agent. The person can be considered morally responsible for the action, deserving praise or blame.

Individuation, principle of – That which makes a thing what it is and not another. See *haecceitas*.

Intellect – One of the soul's powers, the intellect is that by which the human person knows and understands reality. According to Scotus, the intellect operates according to the order of natural or necessary causality.

Intuitive cognition – An unmediated cognitive act, by which the person has a simple, non-judgmental awareness of an object existing and present. Both senses and the intellect are capable of intuitive cognition. Intuitive cognition, unlike abstractive cognition, is certain knowledge, which can refer to internal states ("I doubt" or "I am thinking") as well as to existential awareness of an existing object. Scotus points to intuitive cognition as the experience of the beatific vision, a face-to-face encounter with God.

Irrational potency – A power that is incapable of self-restraint or self-determination. Scotus claims that the intellect is an irrational potency.

Mental species, phantasm – Within the Aristotelian cognitive discussion, this refers to the imaginary representation that the mind produces on the basis of sense experience. Once present, the intelligible species becomes that from which the abstract concept arises through the light of the active (agent) intellect.

Moderate realism – Moderate realism holds that some sort of existence belongs to our concepts and that these concepts map the world in a way that helps the mind know reality.

Nolle – The act of the will by which it rejects (nills) an object.

Non velle – The act of the will by which it refrains from choosing an object.

Order of execution – The sequence of events that flow in a purposeful manner from a rational will. The reverse of the order of intention, since the goal is the last in the order of execution.

Order of intention – The purpose for action. That for which one acts (the goal) is the first in the order of intention, since everything done to reach that goal is done because of the goal.

Order of merit – Established by divine *acceptatio*, this order is defined by charity. It surpasses the moral order and is the order of reward conferred by the divine will.

Potentia absoluta Dei – This refers to all that lies within divine power, bounded only by the principle of non-contradiction. It is what God can do, rather than what God has done.

Potentia ordinata Dei – This refers to what God has done. The natural order God has established. It is often referred to as the "present dispensation."

Potential intellect – The passive dimension to human knowing, it refers to the intellect insofar as it is receptive to the data of sense experience.

Quiddity (quidditas) – Literally, the *whatness* or essence of a thing. For Aristotle, this was the object of intellection, not the particular existing object. The term originated from Arab translators of Aristotle who took the original Greek term, translated it to the Latin *quid quod erat esse* (that which was to be) and then reduced this to a shorthand term, *quidditas*.

Rational potency – A power that acts *with reason*. For Scotus, this is the will.

Suppositum – A general name for a *per se* being which has its ultimate actuality. In the case of a rational or intellectual nature, such a being is called a person. This term is a translation of *hypostasis*, the Greek term used to refer to the persons of the Trinity.

Univocity of being – The concept being *(ens)* is univocal, according to Scotus. This refers to the common, indistinct concept of which the mind is aware in knowing anything at all. *Being* is the most basic and virtual aspect of anything known; it is the *not-nothing*. Scotus affirms that were being not univocal in this way, the human mind would have no natural knowledge of God, nor would Theology have any claim to scientific status.

Velle – The act of the will by which it chooses.

Will –A power of the soul, that by which the person desires and chooses the good. For Scotus, the will alone is the rational potency, since it is capable of self-restraint and self-movement.

Index

Index nominum

Albert the Great 25

Anselm 29, 75, 76, 79, 81, 87, 88, 101, 121, 185, 205, 225, 226

Aristotle 8, 22, 23, 24, 25, 26, 27, 28, 29, 54, 59, 68, 102, 117, 120, 121, 146, 187, 189, 200, 201, 208, 216, 218, 225, 226, 230

Augustine 8, 25, 59, 66, 69, 80, 101, 103, 107, 108, 111, 123, 128, 135, 139, 186, 200, 207, 208

Averroes (Ibn Rushd) 24, 26

Avicenna (Ibn Sina) 25, 153

Boethius 23, 27, 126

Boulnois, Olivier 214, 219

Clare of Assisi 35, 105, 108, 125

Courtenay, William 33

Cross, Richard 101, 214

Dacia, Boethius of 27

Dreyer, Mechthild 102, 214, 215, 216, 218, 219

Dumont, Richard 214, 219

Dumont, Stephen 102, 214, 219, 220

Eustratius 25

Francis of Assisi 9, 11, 39, 45, 66, 75, 77, 100, 105, 108, 119, 125, 146, 147, 148, 149

Frank, William 68, 126, 171, 191, 214, 223

Ghent, Henry of 29, 33, 69, 82, 83, 164, 168

Gonsalves of Spain 16, 17

Heidegger, Martin 40, 41, 149

Honnefelder, Ludger 102, 214, 215, 216, 218, 219

Kenny, Anthony 129, 216, 218

Lombard, Peter 15, 16, 18, 19, 158, 226

Moses Maimonides 24

Noone, Timothy 34, 215, 219

Ockham, William of 13, 30, 31

Osborne, Kenan 126, 132, 223

Pierce, C.S. 68

Plato 24, 25, 120, 166

Rohr, Richard 139, 143

Index rerum